WORLD OF

The Wild West

T15813

Peter Harrison

Consultant: Norman Bancroft Hunt

southwater

This edition is published by Southwater

Southwater is an imprint of
Anness Publishing Limited
Hermes House
88-89 Blackfriars Road
London
SE1 8HA
tel. 020 7401 2077

Distributed in the UK by
The Manning Parnership
251-253 London Road East
Batheaston
Bath BA1 7RL
tel. 01225 852 727
fax 01225 852 852

Distributed in the USA by
Anness Publishing Inc.
27 West 20th Street
Suite 504
New York
NY 10011
tel. 212 807 6739
fax 212 807 6813

Disributed in Australia by
Sandstone Publishing
Unit 1
360 Norton Street
Leichhardt
New South Wales 2040
tel. 02 9560 7888
fax 020 7488

A CIP catalogue record for this book is available from
the British Library

Publisher: Joanna Lorenz
Managing Editor: Gilly Cameron Cooper
Senior Editor: Lisa Miles
Copy Editor: Jackie Gaff
Editorial Reader: Jan Cutler
Series Design: John Jamieson
Designer: Caroline Reeves
Jacket Design: Simon Wilder and Joyce Mason
Illustration: Peter Bull, Stuart Carter, Chris Forsey, Guy
Smith, Clive Spong (Linden Artists), Roger Stewart
(Kevin Jones Associates)
Picture Research: Veneta Bullen
Photography: Paul Bricknell
Stylist: Jane Coney
Production Controller: Don Campaniello

Anness Publishing would like to thank the following
children, and their parents, for modelling for this book:
Michael Ammah, Jake Andrews, Anthony Bainbridge,
Patrick Clifford, Winnie Collate, Joshua Cooper, Molly
Cooper, Emily McGrath, Feroz Mirza, Gigi Playfair and
Tabitha Riley.

PICTURE CREDITS
Front Cover/Back Cover & Endpapers: Peter Newark's
Pictures. The J Allan Cash Library: 38b, 51tr; Sylvia
Bancroft Hunt: 3tl, 5b, 8tl, 8bl, 9tr, 10bl, 11tr, 12tl,
12bl, 13cl, 13bl, 18bl, 37tl, 37tr, 46tl, 55tr; The
Bridgeman Art Library/Museum of North American
Indian: 12br, 13tl; Fort Folle Avoine Information
Centre, Wisconsin: 39tr; Ronald Grant Archives: 4cr,
36bl, 58tc, 59tl, 59tr, 59cl; The Image Bank/David H
Hamilton: 27tr; Bob Langrish: 25cl, 47tr, 47br; Peter
Newark's Pictures: 2br; 3tr; 3br; 4bc; 5tl, 5tr, 5c, 8cr,
9cl, 9br, 13br, 14bl, 16bl, 16cr, 17tl, 17cr, 17br, 20tr,
20bl, 20cr, 21tl, 21tr, 21cr, 22cl, 22br, 23tl, 23tr, 23c,
23br, 24c, 24b, 26bl, 28tr, 28bl, 28br, 29tl, 29tr, 29bl,
34br, 35tr, 36tr, 36cr, 36br, 37br, 37bl, 37tl, 37bl; 42-
43; 44bl; 46cl, 46br, 47c, 48-49, 52-53, 54cl, 54br, 55cl,
55tr, 55br, 56br, 58bl, 58br, 59br; The Specialist
Source/Travel Ink/Ronald Baskin: 4cl, 39cr; /Andrew
Land 21bl; The Stockmarket: 6bl; 17cl.
Previously published in the Discovery series.

CONTENTS

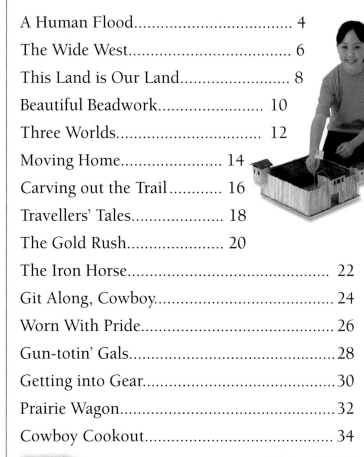

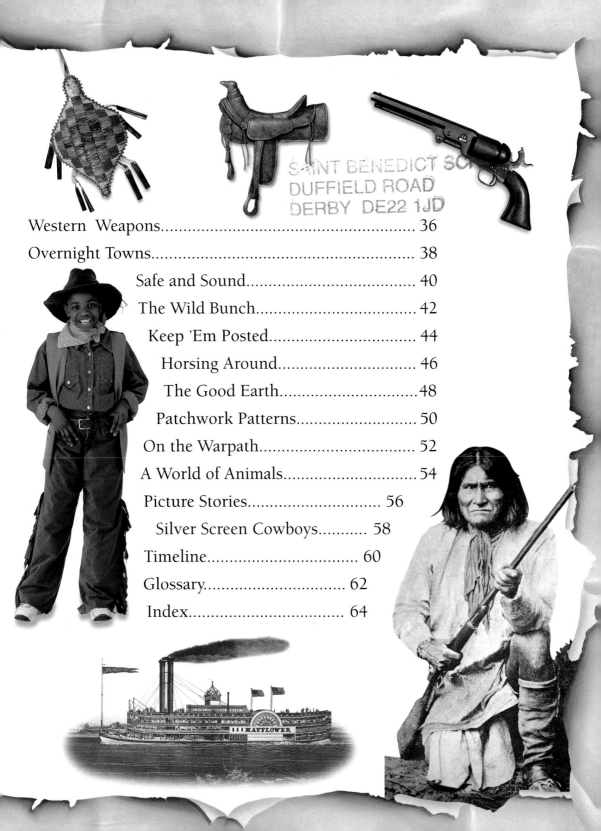

SAINT BENEDICT SC
DUFFIELD ROAD
DERBY DE22 1JD

A Human Flood

▲ **SHELTER WITH THE NATIVES**
An explorer enters a lodge house, the home of a family from the Native American Mandan tribe. He is glad to have found shelter from the snow and the bitter winter winds. The Mandan will give him food and will be able to tell him about the rivers and mountains he has to cross on his journey to come.

Throughout the 1800s, millions of people travelled into the American West. For these newcomers, the land they were journeying into was an unexplored wilderness, and they are known as pioneers, which means "explorer" or "settler". Some pioneers came looking for gold. Others came searching for land they would be able to call their own. They were explorers, fur trappers, missionaries, farmers and cowboys.

Before the pioneers arrived, the West was home to many different tribes of Native Americans. At first, most tribes tried to live peacefully with the newcomers, but fighting broke out after the settlers started to take their land away to build farms, towns and railroads.

The story of the American West is one of bravery, hope and hard work, but it is also one of unhappiness and cruelty.

▲ **STATE OF GROWTH**
These glittering skyscrapers are in Houston, a city in modern-day Texas. By 1990, around 1.6 million people lived in Houston, which was almost the same as the population of the entire State of Texas back in 1880. Texas was one of the first territories in the West to be made a State, in 1845. Hundreds of thousands of cattle were herded from there in the 1870s by cowboys riding the long trail to the railroad.

NO ROOM AT THE TOP ▶
Life in the West brought all kinds of people together. This photograph from the 1939 film *Stagecoach* shows well-bred ladies and gentlemen rubbing shoulders with cowboys, saloon girls, and the roughnecks who drove stagecoaches.

◀ **ALONE AGAIN, NATURALLY**
The fur trappers of the American West were known as mountain men. In the early 1800s, they lived completely alone for months, facing many dangers in unexplored mountain country. Some were savaged by bears. Others suffered frostbite in the freezing cold of winter. One of the most famous mountain men was Kit Carson. Many stories were written about his skill as an explorer, hunter and guide.

▼ HOMELESS AND PENNILESS

A family of Irish farmers is thrown out of its home. Thousands of Scottish and Irish families were made homeless at this time, because the landowners wanted the land. As a result, in the mid-1800s, many people travelled to Canada and the USA to make new lives. In the American West they founded towns, such as McClouth, which were named after Scottish and Irish families. Other immigrants came from all over Europe, looking for land.

▲ STRAIGHT TALKING

The tribes of the West had their own governments, called councils. They met regularly to discuss important problems, such as how to deal with the settlers who arrived in their lands. Chiefs took turns to stand in the middle of a circle, such as the one shown here, and say what they thought. After everyone had spoken, the final decision was based on the opinions of most of the chiefs.

▶ ANGRY YOUNG MEN

A tribe of Native Americans attacks a stagecoach. As the enormous numbers of pioneers tramped across land where the tribes had lived for years, they spoiled the hunting grounds and treated the Native Americans unfairly. Some tribes attacked stagecoaches and wagon trains.

▼ WHERE THE BUFFALO ROAM

Native Americans shared their land with the animals, such as this herd of buffalo, which lived there. They hunted animals for food, but because there were not many tribes, the animals' way of life was not damaged. When hundreds of thousands of settlers began arriving, it affected the animals badly. Farmers saw many of the animals as pests and killed them.

The Wide West

The American West was an enormous area of land which included mountains, deserts and a vast grassland region called the Great Plains. The American West stretched from the Mississippi River in the East to the Rocky Mountains in the West. In the north it began in the modern provinces of Alberta and Saskatchewan in Canada and ended in present-day northern Mexico.

At the time of the first pioneers, it could take more than four months to travel across the West by wagon train. After the first east-to-west-coast railroad was completed in 1869, people could speed from New York to San Francisco in just ten days. As more farms and towns grew up, the Native Americans of the West were forced by the United States government to live in smaller and smaller areas to make room for all the settlers.

▲ BREATH-TAKING BARRIERS

The Rocky Mountains run for almost 5,000km, from Canada in the north to New Mexico in the south. For settlers on their way to new homes in States such as Oregon, the Rockies were their greatest physical challenge. It was almost impossible to take wagons high up into the mountains at any time of year. Settlers had to use the lower mountain passes. If travellers reached the mountains in winter, deep snow and intense cold made it very difficult to continue.

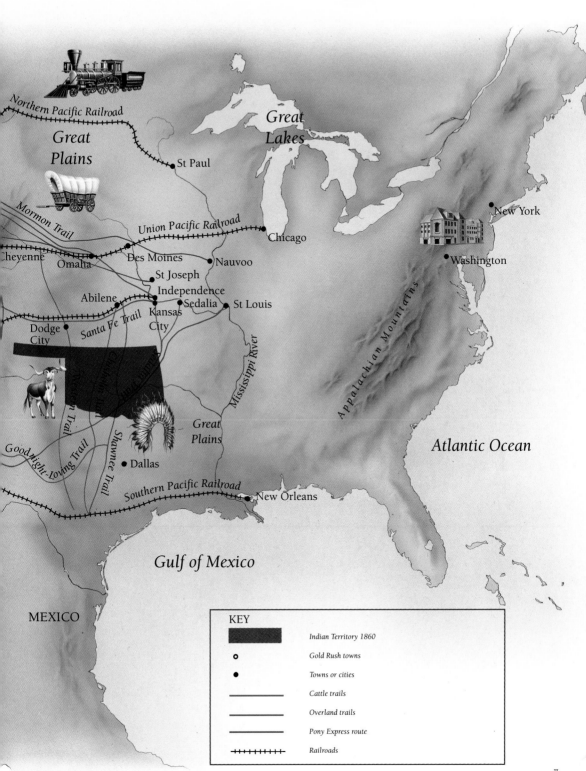

Northern Pacific Railroad

Great
Plains

Mormon Trail

Union Pacific Railroad

Great
Lakes

St Paul

Chicago

Cheyenne

Omaha

Des Moines

Nauvoo

St Joseph

Abilene

Independence

Sedalia

St Louis

Kansas
City

Dodge
City

Santa Fe Trail

Mississippi River

Chisholm Trail

Goodnight-Loving Trail

Shawnee Trail

Great
Plains

Dallas

New York

Washington

Appalachian Mountains

Atlantic Ocean

Southern Pacific Railroad

New Orleans

Gulf of Mexico

MEXICO

KEY

Indian Territory 1860

Gold Rush towns

Towns or cities

Cattle trails

Overland trails

Pony Express route

Railroads

This Land is Our Land

Many different Native American tribes lived in the West, and their way of life was suited to the land they lived on – river valleys and tree-covered mountains, the wide open grasslands of the Great Plains, or the dry, dusty deserts. The land was not damaged or polluted because it was not overcrowded, and the tribes respected the land.

In the mountains and rivers of the North-west region, in what are now the States of Montana, Idaho and Oregon, lived such tribes as the Nez Percé, Shoshoni and Modoc. Fishing was an important part of their way of life. The tribes of the Great Plains, such as the Sioux, Cheyenne and Arapaho were hunters and riders who followed the paths of the buffalo. The region south of the Great Plains, in what is now New Mexico and Arizona, is one of deserts and canyons. The tribes who lived there, such as the Navajo, Apache and Pueblo, farmed beans, maize (corn), and squash.

▲ **CHIEF BACON FAT**
This chief was a member of the Osage tribe. He wears tattoo markings, showing that he was a warrior responsible for tribal traditions. Religious dances, songs and stories were very important to Native Americans.

◄ **CHOICE OF CHIEFS**
Pehriska-Rupa was a member of the Hidatsa tribe which lived in three villages on the northern Plains. Unlike the Sioux and Cheyenne, who moved across the Plains all year round, the Hidatsa stayed in their villages, although the men did hunt buffalo. The women grew crops such as maize, beans and squash.

▲ **DANCE OF STRENGTH**
Members of the Mandan tribe danced and sang to communicate with the spirit of the buffalo. They believed they could gain strength and success in hunting through these ceremonies. Karl Bodmer, a Swiss artist who travelled among the tribes of the Great Plains, painted this buffalo dance in the 1830s.

▼ PAINTED HOME

Decorated with hunting and fighting scenes, this tepee belongs to a family of the Crow tribe. The Crow lived on the Great Plains and were famous as warriors. Later, they became scouts for the United States Army. Although they lived mainly by hunting, the Crow also grew tobacco.

▲ DESERT HIGH-RISES

In early times, tribes of the South-west region built villages like this one high up in the cliff faces of canyons. The villages were very carefully constructed and had complex layouts. Many of these villages were deserted around the year 1350. Even today, experts are unsure why they were abandoned.

CIRCLE OF THE WORLD ▼

This hoop was used in dance ceremonies by members of the Cree tribe who lived on the Great Plains, and hunted buffalo. There were also Cree living farther north, in what is now Canada. They lived in woodlands and hunted beaver and moose. This dance hoop is divided into the four quarters into which all Native Americans believed the world was divided. The feathers are symbols of the spirits that Native Americans believed had created the world.

▲ MOTHER AND CHILD

The Navajo are the largest Native American tribe in the present-day US. They live in their traditional lands in New Mexico and Arizona. It is difficult to farm this very dry, desert country and so many Navajo now work in cities such as Los Angeles to earn money and can only spend some of the time on their own lands.

Beautiful Beadwork

The Native Americans of the West were not only hunters and warriors, they were also artists and craftworkers. This project shows you how to make two pieces of jewellery similar to the designs created by Native Americans.

Because they did not live in the kind of society that has shops and industries, Native American men and women made everything they needed themselves, from clothes and blankets, to tools and weapons. Many objects were richly decorated. Before settlers came to their lands, Native Americans used porcupine quills for this. They treated the quills to soften them, then dyed them different colours and wove them into beautiful designs.

The settlers brought coloured glass beads with them to the West. The tribespeople bargained with traders for the beads, among other things, and developed great skill in using them to make brilliant, richly coloured patterns on dresses, trousers, shoes and many other possessions.

You will need: 75cm of narrow leather thong; scissors; 2m of strong, waxed thread; selection of glass and silver beads in different sizes; four brightly coloured, dyed feathers; four beads – must have big enough holes to cover the knotted leather thong.

1 Cut two strips of leather thong, 15cm long. You will use these strips to tie your finished necklace around your neck.

2 Next, take the waxed thread and cut off one long piece, 25cm long. Then cut four short pieces, each 10cm long.

6 Thread on your smaller beads, covering only half of each piece of waxed thread. Tie a knot in each thread to secure the beads.

7 Tie each feathery piece on to the main necklace. Then tie on the second leather thong at the free end and cover the knot with a bead.

Native American shoes like these are called moccasins. The tribes of the Great Plains made them from a piece of dried buffalo hide (skin) which was folded into a shape that wrapped around the foot. Moccasins were often decorated with coloured patterns of quills or beads.

11 Take the knotted end of the threads and tie on one of the leather strips. Cover the whole knot with a large bead.

12 Thread beads on one of the five pieces of waxed thread. Leave a space about 3cm long at the end of the thread.

3 Knot one end of one of the leather strips to one end of the 25cm-long waxed thread. Thread on a bead to cover the knot.

4 Thread your larger beads on to the long piece of waxed thread, until there is about a 10cm space left at the end of it.

5 Now make the dangling pieces of the necklace. For each one, tie one end of a short piece of waxed thread around the quill of a feather.

Decorations were hung on the cradles of Native American babies, for the baby to enjoy and to protect it from harmful spirits. The cradle decoration above is made from deerskin with porcupine quill embroidery. Inside, it contains the baby's umbilical cord, which joined the baby to the mother when the baby was in the womb.

8 To make a bracelet, cut two 20cm-long strips of leather thong. You will use these to tie the bracelet around your wrist.

9 Next, cut five lengths of waxed thread, each about 20cm long. These threads will form the main, beaded part of your bracelet.

10 Take the five pieces of waxed thread, and make a big knot at one end to tie them all together.

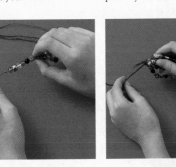

13 Knot the end of the thread to secure the beads. Then bead and knot each of the other four pieces of waxed thread.

14 Knot all five ends of the waxed threads together. Lastly, tie on the last leather strip and cover the knot with a large bead.

You can often see jewellery like this on sale in the western USA. Today's Native Americans make it for the tourist trade. It is based on materials and designs that they have been used for centuries.

Three Worlds

The Native Americans of the West all believed the world was full of spirits who lived in every part of nature – in animals, plants, rivers, the rain, the sun and the stars. Some tribes, such as the Sioux, believed in a single great spirit whom they called Wakan Tanka. Communicating with the spirits was very important for all tribes. To do this they had many ceremonies. Often these were dances at which people dressed to look like a spirit and when songs were sung about the spirit and the tribe.

For Native Americans, there were three worlds that existed all at the same time – a watery underworld, the earth itself, and the sky. Particular people in each tribe had special powers for understanding and talking to the spirits, by going into a trance (sleep-like state) and having visions. These people were called medicine men, or shamans. They cured illness and gave advice to the tribes about how to respect the spirits. Young men growing to adulthood also went into trances to meet the spirits. While in a trance, they experienced spiritual journeys, called vision quests. They returned with messages from the spirits that told them the kind of adult they would become.

▲ **SPIRIT OF CHILDHOOD**
Children of the South-west Pueblo tribes were given dolls like this one to remind them of the spirits. The spirits were called kachinas, and so the dolls have become known as kachina dolls. The Pueblo tribes believed that their crops were protected by the kachina spirits.

▲ **PULLING POWER**
A medicine man of the Blackfoot tribe wears an animal-skin cloak as a sign that he lives close to the spirit world. The action of shaking the tambourine called the spirits to him. Sky gods came to him through the arrow shape in his other hand.

▲ **STORY TELLING**
A story painted on a deerskin tells how a special group within the Hopi tribe of the South-west, the snake clan, learned how to speak to the snake god and to understand him. Spirit dances were also ways of telling stories about the tribe and of recounting what the gods had said to the tribe in the past.

◄ TEST OF ENDURANCE

To prove their bravery, men of the Mandan tribe have pierced the skin of their chests with skewers. They are hanging from the roof of their lodge by rawhide strips. They are taking part in their O-Kee-Pa ceremony, which the tribe held every year. The ceremony lasted for four days. The Mandan believed that, long ago, the world had been covered by a great flood and only one man had survived. During the O-Kee-Pa ceremony, dances and songs were performed to please the spirits and make sure that the great flood would never happen again. The ceremony was also a special time when the young men of the tribe mutilated and tested themselves in the way shown in this drawing, to prove that they were strong.

◄ TEPEE SPIRITS

The tepee of the tribe's medicine man was often painted with images of the spirits of animals. The tribe believed that this would bring them success in their hunting expeditions. This tepee belongs to people from the modern Blackfoot tribe. They have decorated it in the same tradition as their grandparents and great-grandparents.

▲ SINGING TO THE DEAD

After so many of their people had died in wars with the government, Native Americans began to believe that a spirit would come to save them. They began to dance a ritual they called the Ghost Dance, shown in this drawing. They believed that the Ghost Dance would make the dead people killed in wars, and also the dead buffalo, come back to life again.

▲ FLY LIKE A BIRD

This cap from the Apache tribe is decorated with hawk and owl feathers. Native Americans believed that all animals had spirit powers and that they could share in these powers.

Moving Home

Although some Native Americans stayed in one place and lived in permanent houses, many of the Plains tribes were travellers who followed and hunted the buffalo herds. Their movable homes are called tepees. They were made from wooden poles and buffalo hides, and sometimes decorated.

After the settlers arrived in the West, the US government started to build military forts on the Great Plains. Native Americans sometimes camped nearby in order to trade with the newcomers.

This project shows you how to make a model of a Native American tepee and campsite.

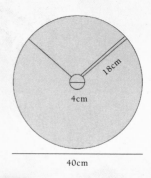

18cm

4cm

40cm

1 Following the basic measurements shown above, copy the template for the tepee cover on to the piece of chamois leather, using a ruler and pair of compasses.

You will need: ruler; pair of compasses; pen; chamois leather, 50 x 50cm; cardboard, 100 x 100cm; scissors; saucer; 12 wooden kebab sticks, cut to 12cm long; piece of string, 25cm long; household (PVA) glue; 2 shades of green, red and brown poster paint; paintbrush; air-drying modelling clay; three cocktail sticks; fine sand; sponge.

6 Following the template again, cut the triangular segment and the central hole out of the chamois leather tepee cover.

7 Trim the string at the top of the sticks so that it doesn't hang down. Spread household glue evenly over the outer edges of the sticks.

8 Wrap the leather around the sticks, pressing it firmly on to each one. Fold back the overlapping flap and leave the tepee to dry.

This painting shows a Plains family on the move. The horse in the foreground is pulling a framework called a travois. Packed on the travois are the family's tepee and all their goods and possessions. Before the Plains tribes had horses, they used dogs to pull loads from one camp to another.

11 To make the camp fire, cut a flat circle out of modelling clay. Roll small balls of clay to use as stones around the edge.

12 Stick the cocktail sticks into the modelling clay to form a tripod over the fire. Leave it to dry, then paint it.

2 Cut out a piece of cardboard to use as the base. Use the shape shown above as a guide. It should measure at least 80 x 90cm.

3 Draw around an upturned saucer to make a circle on the cardboard. With a ruler, draw lines to divide the circle into eight equal segments.

4 Make a hole at each point of the circle. Place a kebab stick in each hole and tie them 4cm from the top. Glue the sticks to the base.

5 Using scissors, cut around the edge of the circle that you have drawn on the chamois leather. This will become the tepee covering.

9 Cut 3cm lengths from the sharp ends of the last four kebab sticks. Push them through the leather to peg the top of the tepee together.

10 Now that your tepee is finished, you can decorate the base. Give the cardboard a light covering of green poster paint.

Most people's tepees were left plain, but the chief's was often decorated with painted patterns. If you would like to, you could use fabric marker pens to decorate your tepee. Or, you could make a larger campsite with several tepees, including a decorated one for the chief.

13 Spread the base with glue, then finely sprinkle the sand over it to give it some texture. Shake off the excess sand.

14 Tear a few small lumps from the sponge to use as bushes. Paint them different shades of green. Dry, then stick them to the base.

Carving out the Trail

There were already European mountain men, travellers and missionaries west of the Mississippi River in the 1700s, but the territory claimed by the US government did not reach as far as this. Then in 1803 it bought the Louisiana Territory, a vast area of land beyond the Mississippi, from the French emperor Napoleon. After an expedition was sent to explore the new land, pioneers followed in the explorers' footsteps and carved out trails that others could follow. Further south, the USA fought with Mexico, and by 1848 had taken from it a huge chunk of land, including the area that was to become the States of California and Texas.

The US government in the East encouraged settlers to move westward. Many people, such as the followers of the Mormon religion, did this to escape persecution. Others went in search of gold, which was discovered in California in 1848. Most of the people who travelled into the West, however, were simply looking for land to claim as their own.

▲ WAGONS ROLLING

A wagon train bumps and rolls along the overland trail to Oregon. Clouds of dust are kicked up by the oxen's feet far into the distance. The trail was 3,200km long and it took around four months to do the journey.

◄ MAN OF THE WILD

Joe Meek became a fur trapper when he was 19 and spent 11 years travelling the West from north to south. He married a woman of the Nez Percé tribe. Mountain men like Joe Meek brought their furs back from the wilderness once a year, to be traded at a camp near St Louis, Missouri.

▲ GUIDING LIGHT

The image in this painting is the guiding force that many pioneers believed led them westward. They called it Manifest Destiny, which means "proof of fate". The government thought that filling the land with farms and towns was its duty, because the USA needed to grow larger.

◀ ON THE FREEDOM TRAIL

Members of the Mormon faith on the journey they made into the West in 1847. They were on their way to found a new community in the Great Salt Lake valley, Utah. Many of them carry all their possessions on handcarts because they are too poor to buy wagons. The Mormons were forced to travel more than 2,000km from Nauvoo, Illinois in the East after people there attacked them for their beliefs. People were also suspicious of the important part Mormons were playing in State politics. In 1844, this had led to the Mormon leader, Joseph Smith, being shot and killed by a mob.

▲ RESTING ON THE TRAIL

These settlers on the trail westward have unhitched their oxen from their wagons and are resting. Often, when the sun was high in the middle of the day, it was too hot to carry on walking alongside the wagon, so wagon trains stopped to give everyone a chance to gather more energy for the rest of the day's journey.

▲ CITY OF THE SAINTS

The modern Mormon Temple in Salt Lake City, Utah, is the international centre for the Mormon faith, to which millions of people now belong. The largest Mormon sect (religious group) was founded by Joseph Smith in 1830 and is called the Church of Jesus Christ of Latter-day Saints. Salt Lake City became wealthy and successful in the 1860s, as the railroads developed and people mined the valuable mineral deposits in rocks around the city.

THE LAND OF THE FREE ▶

A family of African-Americans poses in front of their new home in the State of Nebraska, central USA, in 1887. The Civil War of 1861–65 freed the African-Americans of the South from slavery. Freed slaves did not have enough money to buy land for themselves in the South, though, so many of them travelled into the West, where land was cheaper.

Travellers' Tales

Before the 1800s, few white Americans had travelled into the West. The first people to explore the region went on their own or in small groups. As they journeyed, they often made rough maps of the rivers, mountains and forests they came across. Like the settlers who followed in their footsteps, many explorers also kept journals (diaries) describing what happened to them.

This project shows you how to make a journal of your own, which you can use to record a journey or a holiday. Afterwards, your friends and family will be able to read about where you have been.

In 1804, explorers William Clark and Meriwether Lewis led an expedition into the vast region between the Mississippi River and the Pacific Ocean. They brought back a great deal of new information. New maps of the West were drawn, showing where rivers and mountains were, their height and length, and the distances between them. This kind of information made it easier for settlers to travel westward in the years that followed.

You will need: cardboard, 40 x 30cm; ruler; pencil; scissors; pad of white drawing paper, at least 45 x 30cm; tea bag; water; paintbrush; coffee granules; brown embroidery thread; needle; household (PVA) glue; hessian fabric, 55 x 35cm; masking tape.

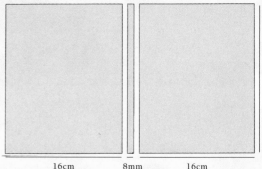

16cm   8mm   16cm   21cm

1 Using the measurements above, copy the shapes on to the piece of cardboard. Then cut out the pieces – these will form the spine and covers of your journal.

6 Fold the large piece of paper into three equal parts. The part on the right will be a fold-out section in the middle of your journal.

7 Keeping the fold-out to the right, put the largest piece of paper on top of the other six. Use running stitch to sew them together.

The State of Wyoming is in the central northern part of the USA, and many wagon trains crossed it on the Oregon Trail and the Mormon Trail. The land is mountainous, particularly in the western part where it reaches the foothills of the Rocky Mountains. It is a very high region, so nights were cold for people sleeping on the ground next to their wagons.

10 Tie a knot at the top of three 40cm strands of thread. Tape them on to a work surface and plait them, finishing with a knot.

2 On the white paper, use a ruler and pencil to mark out six 30 x 20cm small rectangles. Also mark out a larger, 45 x 20cm rectangle.

3 Cut out all seven pieces of paper, then fold the six rectangles in half. You will use these for the pages of your travel journal.

4 Put the tea bag in cold water and stir it around. After the water has coloured, paint it lightly on all seven pieces of paper with a brush.

5 Sprinkle all the paper with a few coffee granules. Leave them for 5 minutes, then shake them off. Leave the paper to dry.

8 Spread glue on one side of the cardboard pieces. Press the glued sides on the hessian, as above. Trim the fabric, leaving a 2cm border.

9 Cut the four corners off the hessian, as shown above. Spread glue lightly on the hessian border and press it down over the cardboard.

Settlers would have been familiar with some of the landmarks they saw on their journey from guidebook descriptions and magazines. They also recorded details of their own travels in their journals, as they went along. You could use your journal either as a diary or as a scrapbook, sticking in a collection of photographs or souvenirs to remind you of a holiday. You could draw a big picture or map on the fold-out section in the middle of the journal.

11 Tape the plaited bookmark to one side of the spine. Glue the back of the first and last journal pages inside the covers.

SETTLER'S STORY

Philura Vanderburgh was 13 years old when she travelled West in 1864. Here is an extract from her story.
"Long before daylight one morning, we filled every available water carrier...and trailed off through the weird darkness...We were starting across a desert, seventy miles without water. In two days we were to cross thirty-five miles a day, fifteen miles further than our average distance. It was to be two long and terrible drives..."

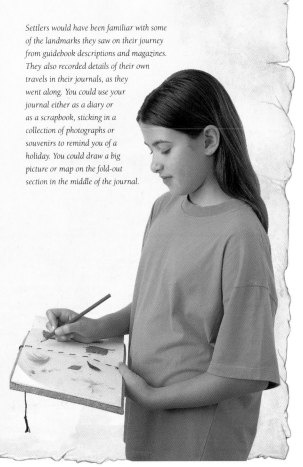

The Gold Rush

Tens of thousands of people hurried west to California after gold was found there in 1848. These gold prospectors (hunters) called themselves the Forty-niners, because they arrived in California in 1849. When miners found gold, they said that they had "hit pay dirt".

The Forty-niners were not the first people to look for gold in the West. In the 1500s, Spanish explorers travelled up from Central America into what is today New Mexico and Kansas. They were looking for what they called Cibolla, or the Seven Cities of Gold. They were unsuccessful.

By 1900, gold had also been discovered in what is now Montana, Wyoming, Colorado and Nevada. Each discovery was followed by a gold rush, with thousands of people racing to the site and hunting furiously for gold. They hoped they could become rich just by digging it from the ground. Some people did become wealthy, but many others gained little or nothing for their trouble.

▲ ALL PANNED OUT
A prospector pans for gold. The method was called panning because it involved a metal pan, and it was one of the simplest ways of looking for gold. Mud from the river bank or bed was put into the pan, then water was poured on and swirled around it. If there was gold in the mud, it would settle at the bottom of the pan to be seen when the prospector poured off the mixture of water and sandy river mud.

◄ WISH YOU WERE HERE
The Forty-niners were proud of having travelled such great distances to join the Californian gold rush, and had photographs taken to send back to the folks at home. This Forty-niner has a pickaxe over one shoulder, a gold pan in one hand, and a hoe in the other. The sack on his lap shows how much gold he has found – or the amount he is pretending to have found!

▲ SHIP-SHAPE SETTLERS
Scores of ships pack San Francisco Harbour in 1849, bringing prospectors to join the Californian gold rush. Many miners travelled to the West by ship, instead of making the difficult, 3,400km journey over land. In three years, the gold rush boosted the population of San Francisco from only 14,000 to almost 250,000.

▲ WATER POWER

A miner uses a jet of water from a hose to wash soil and rock out of a hillside. The loose soil was then put through a wooden device called a separating cradle, which separated out any gold from the soil. When all the gold near the surface had been found, mining became harder and more advanced machinery was needed.

▲ RUSH OF FEAR

Thousands of Chinese men took part in the Californian gold rush, travelling by ship halfway across the world from their homeland. When California became a State in 1850, some white American miners said the Chinese had no right to dig for gold there and attacked them, killing many of the men.

◄ SAFE PLACE

An office of Wells Fargo, a banking and transport company that grew up during the gold rush. In the early years, gold dealers often cheated prospectors by giving them less money than the gold was really worth. The Wells Fargo company was more honest, and a safer place for miners to sell their gold. The company still exists today.

◄ BOOM TOWN

Mining towns sprang up overnight as soon as gold or silver was discovered nearby. Bodie became a boom town in 1877 after gold was discovered in the high, desert country of north California. It was a wild place. Killings were a daily occurrence, and robberies, stage holdups and street fights were also a regular part of life. Whisky was brought to the town in carriages, 100 barrels at a time.

NEXT STOP CHEYENNE!

Riding on the Union Pacific railroad, men, women and children are travelling to San Francisco to make new homes in the West. The conductor walks along the carriage calling, "Next stop Cheyenne!". It took eight days to travel from East to West. The seats were hard wooden benches, and cooking and toilet facilities were basic. The wealthy could travel in more luxurious cars.

The Iron Horse

To make travel into the West faster and easier, the US government decided to encourage the building of a railway across the entire continent. It took thousands of workers seven years to construct the line joining the Missouri River in the East to the Pacific Ocean in the West. They laid tracks across deserts, blasted tunnels through mountainsides, and raised bridge after bridge over the many rivers the line had to cross. The railway was completed in 1869, and by 1883 it had been followed by three more – the Atlantic and Pacific, the Southern Pacific, and the Northern Pacific.

The railways brought benefits to the new settlers, but they were also the cause of bitter fighting. The tracks sliced through Native American tribal land, and the construction crews often came under attack. To make matters worse, the US government had given the railway companies land adjoining the track, which they then sold to settlers. As more and more people came to live on their land, the tribes grew more and more angry.

◄ COMIN' THROUGH

Between 1860–61, the Pony Express company employed riders to carry mail as fast as they could across the continent. It was the first attempt to link the east and west coasts. The riders galloped as fast as they could between stops called staging posts. There were almost a hundred staging posts, and the 3,200km journey took about ten days. However, the Pony Express only lasted for 18 months, because it was such an expensive way to cover the distance. One of its early riders was William F Cody. He later became famous as Buffalo Bill, leader of the Wild West shows.

OLE MAN RIVER ►

The Mayflower, painted in 1855, was one of the many steamboats that once sailed up and down the Mississippi River between New Orleans in the South and St Louis in the North. For almost 50 years, from the 1830s onward, steamboats were the most efficient way of carrying goods and people in the central USA. However, the railroads began to take away trade because they were faster, and by the 1880s steamboats were being used less and less.

▲ No Competition

Although the railroad was faster, a wagon train was cheaper and more practical for ordinary settlers. Trains were fine if you had only one suitcase, but they were a very expensive way of moving all the possessions you needed to set up a new home in the West.

▲ East Meets West

The Union Pacific Railroad was built in two halves, with one track running from Nebraska in the East, and the second from California in the West. Promontory, in what is now the State of Utah, was where the two railway tracks and their locomotives finally met in May 1869. To celebrate the finishing of this first transcontinental railway, a golden spike was struck into the track.

◀ Killing Time

Some railway travellers passed the time on the long, transcontinental journey by shooting any buffalo that came near the train. This killing for the sake of killing was acceptable at the time, but it helped to cause a massive decline of the buffalo. Travelling by train was boring and uncomfortable. Carriages were narrow and crowded, and it was difficult to get up and walk around.

Smokestack Lightning ▶

The great benefit of the railroads was that they linked up the towns in the huge, open spaces of the West. The plume of smoke belching out of a train's smokestack could be seen for a great distance across the countryside. It was a welcome sign for people living in remote towns far from the nearest city. It meant that they were not alone – the train was coming. This print of an express train was published in 1864.

Git Along, Cowboy

The cowboys of the West were often in charge of as many as 2,000 cattle. Most cattle were young males, known as steers. Cowboys had to drive these huge herds hundreds of kilometres north, from the cattle ranches of Texas to the railroad stations in States such as Kansas. From there, the cattle were shipped on trains to the East for food.

Moving large herds of cattle northwards began in the 1870s. The animals were driven along trails with names such as the Chisholm Trail and the Goodnight-Loving Trail. At the end of the trails, railroad towns such as Abilene and Dodge City sprang up overnight. There, cattle sellers and buyers met and struck deals. By the end of the 1880s, the railroads had extended nearer to the cattle ranches. There was no longer any need to ride out on the trail, driving large herds. Those days were at an end.

▲ RUNAWAY STEER
A steer has broken away from the herd. The cowboy throws his lasso, trying to drop the noose around the steer's horns. The steer is running fast, but the cowboy is an experienced cowhand – he'll rope this runaway in.

THE LONG AND WINDING TRAIL ▶
The Great Plains are wide and flat, and if a cowboy looked back at the trail behind him, he might have seen a line of thousands of cattle stretching right to the horizon. Keeping the cattle in line was one of a cowboy's most important tasks. None of the animals could be allowed to stray and get lost, or the ranch owner would have lost money.

COWBOY AT WORK ▶
Cowboys had tough lives, and wore tough, practical clothes. This cowboy wears a gun at his belt and carries a rope lasso, or lariat, for roping steers.

plaited leather quirt for whipping his horse on

leather chaps, worn over trousers, for protection

high-heeled boots and spurs

MEXICAN VAQUEROS ▶
Mexican cowboys watch as a herd of horses is rounded up into a fenced area known as a corral. Mexican cowboys are called *vaqueros*, and the cowboys of the American West copied and adapted much of their equipment, making the *vaqueros'* big sombrero hats smaller, and using similar roping techniques.

◄ IN YOUR DREAMS

Action-packed paintings such as this one created a myth about cowboys that lasted a long time after all the real cowboys were dead and gone. It was painted by Charles M Russell in 1904, 20 years after the cattle trails had stopped being used. In real life, three riders would never have been allowed to chase after a single runaway steer. It would have been a waste of manpower. Every single cowboy had more than enough to do on the trail.

ALL DRESSED UP ►

This is Isom Dart, an African-American cowboy of the 1870s. He has dressed up for this photograph in a smart jacket, hat, necktie and chaps. He's wearing a pair of pistols at his belt. Many cowboys were African-American or Mexican in origin, although they are usually portrayed in the movies as white Americans.

▲ DUDE RANCH

The myth of the cowboy is still very powerful. Some people today, many of whom spend their lives working in offices, dream about the cowboy's life being free and easy. These riders trekking through the desert are on a dude ranch, a modern ranch where people from the city pay to spend a holiday riding a horse, roping cattle and imagining that they are living the life of a cowboy.

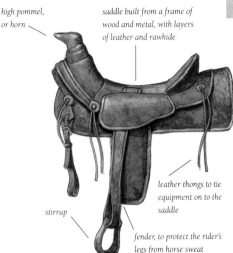

high pommel, or horn

saddle built from a frame of wood and metal, with layers of leather and rawhide

leather thongs to tie equipment on to the saddle

stirrup

fender, to protect the rider's legs from horse sweat

◄ IN THE SADDLE

Cowboys used a special saddle. The pommel at the front of the saddle is raised up and shaped like a hook, unlike the usual horse-riding saddle. The cowboy used the pommel for tying one end of the lasso when roping cattle. He could then use his horse's weight to pull against the steer's weight to stop it from moving.

Worn With Pride

In the West, sheriffs and other lawmen wore a metal star pinned on the front of their jackets to identify themselves. It was their job to keep law and order. The first project here shows you how to make your own sheriff's badge.

Cowboys lived most of their lives far from towns. If they needed anything, such as a rope or a fence, they had to make it themselves. They wove strips of rawhide into ropes, whips, hatbands and belts. Every belt needs a buckle to hold it together, and one way a cowboy could get a new one was to win it as a prize at a special cowboy contest called a rodeo. The rider that could stay on a bucking horse or steer the longest might be given a special belt buckle. Wearing this would show his friends how skilful he was as a cowboy.

The second project here shows you how to make a prize belt buckle of your own.

You will need: 1 medium block air-drying modelling clay; rolling pin; star-shaped pastry cutter, 10cm in diameter; household (PVA) glue; kebab stick or pencil; plastic flowerpot, 20cm in diameter; modelling tool; large safety pin with flat plate (from a craft shop); 2 strips of bias binding tape, 8cm long; needle; cotton; silver poster paint; paintbrush; black permanent marker pen.

This saloon near the Pecos River in New Mexico was the court of Judge Roy Bean. He became famous for dispensing justice in the 1880s and 1890s even though he knew nothing about the law. It was a wild place and he called himself 'The Only Law West of the Pecos'. Once he even fined a dead man 40 dollars for carrying a concealed weapon.

1 Use the rolling pin to roll a handful of the modelling clay out into two clay circles. Each circle should be about 5mm thick.

2 With the star-shaped pastry cutter, press out a star from one of the clay circles. Lift the star carefully from the surrounding clay.

5 To give the star a curved shape, press it on to the side of the flowerpot. Peel the star away gently. Put it aside to dry for 24 hours.

6 Use the modelling tool to cut out a rectangular shape with rounded corners, as shown. It should measure about 8 x 5cm.

10 After 24 hours, when the star is dry, glue the plate of the safety pin to the back of the star. Attach it to the flat space in the middle.

11 When the buckle is dry, glue two strips of bias binding tape across the back. Use a running stitch to sew them into two loops.

3 Roll some modelling clay to make six tiny balls. Each one should be about half as big as a fingernail. Glue one on each point of the star.

4 With the kebab stick, or the point of a pencil, make a line of tiny dots around the edge of the star. Do this as neatly as you can.

Prize belt buckles were meant to be seen, so they were usually made big and obvious. This cowboy's buckle features a rearing bronco, or wild horse. This image tells everyone that he is a tough cowboy who won't let any horses get the better of him. He is wearing the buckle with a braided belt.

7 Follow step 3 again to make 12 more tiny modelling clay balls. Then glue the balls around the edge of the buckle.

8 With the kebab stick, or the point of a pencil, decorate the parts of the buckle between the balls with dots or little swirls.

9 Follow step 5 again to give the buckle a curved shape. Make sure you lift it off gently, then put it aside to dry for 24 hours.

12 Once the glue you used on the badge and the buckle is completely dry, you can paint them both with the silver paint.

13 The finishing touch is to use a black pen to decorate them. Draw a star in the middle of the badge and the buckle.

Thread a thick leather belt through the loops on the back of your buckle and pin on your sheriff's badge – you're ready to hunt down those outlaws!

27

Gun-totin' Gals

Women in the West led many different kinds of lives. For white and African-American female farmers, all sorts of skills went into running a home and raising children, from growing food, to weaving cloth and making it into clothes. Other women lived in towns, where they ran hotels, stores, laundries or post offices, or they worked as missionaries, dressmakers or singers. Many, such as the Mormon, Emmeline Wells, also campaigned for women's right to vote.

Native American women also needed special skills, including weaving baskets and making decorations from quills and beads. The women of some tribes built houses out of turf sods (slabs of grass and earth). Other women of the West, such as Calamity Jane, became famous because their lives were unusual for the time. Dahteste, a Mescalero Apache woman, was a skilled rider and hunter. She learned English and was a valued negotiator between the Apache and the US Cavalry.

▲ BUFFALO SKIN

The Native American women on the left of this painting are stretching a buffalo hide to dry in the sun. After they killed a buffalo, Native Americans removed its skin. The dried leather had many uses, including making tepee covers, clothes and bags. Before the skins could be used, they had to be scraped clean of all meat and dried. This work was a special skill practised by the women of the tribes.

◀ TOUGH GIRL JANE

Calamity Jane was a woman of the West who had a reputation for being as tough as any man. She wore men's clothes, carried a gun, and smoked and drank a lot. She was born Martha Jane Cannary in 1852 and, according to one legend, her nickname came from the way she warned men that to offend her was to court calamity (meaning disaster). She was an expert at shooting and riding, and appeared in travelling Wild West shows.

▲ CHARLEY PARKHURST

A few women, in order to live a freer life, pretended to be men. Cigar-smoking and whisky-drinking stagecoach driver, Charley Parkhurst was discovered to be a woman only on 'his' death in 1879. There were also cases of women going to war dressed as men.

▲ BANDIT BELLE

Belle Starr did not become famous until after she was killed in 1889, and her story was told in many dime novels (cheap story books). During her life she was married to two outlaws – first James Reed, and then after Reed's death, Sam Starr. Belle and Sam's cabin was used as a hideout by outlaws such as Jesse James, and Belle herself organized many robberies, but she only ever spent six months in prison. She died after being shot in the back by another outlaw.

▲ LITTLE SURE SHOT

Annie Oakley became world-famous after she began working with Buffalo Bill's Wild West Show in 1885. The show included shooting and riding displays and a mock battle with Native Americans, and it toured the USA and Europe. Annie first learned to shoot when she was only six years old. By the time she was 15, she was better than any man she knew. One of her tricks was to shoot the ash off the end of a cigarette while someone was smoking it.

◄ A WOMAN'S LIFE OF TOIL

Many women of the West were like those in this photograph of a group of Scandinavian settlers. They came from Europe and did not speak English. They had little money and no idea what to expect when they travelled westward. For women such as these, life was a long, hard struggle with the difficulties of raising a family on a farm in the middle of nowhere. Many died in childbirth or from illness, because there was very little medical care.

Getting into Gear

A cowboy might ride his horse for 16 or more hours every day, so his clothes had to be very practical. This project shows you how to make two key items – a hat and a pair of chaps.

A cowboy's hat was usually made from a type of hard-wearing wool called felt. A wide brim stopped the sun shining into his eyes as he rode. The hat could also be used to signal to other cowboys and to hold water for horses. Chaps protected a cowboy's legs from the horns of the cattle he drove, and from being burned by the rope he used to lasso them. His strong leather boots had pointed toes and high heels because these helped to keep his feet in the stirrups (the loops hanging from straps on either side of the saddle).

You will need: tape measure; paper for the templates; pen; scissors; 1.5m piece of brown material for each chap; 1.5m of brown felt for hat; pins; needle; brown embroidery thread; stiffening fabric, 1m; 3 balls of thick wool in three colours; masking tape.

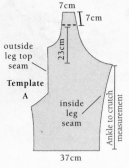

7cm | 7cm
outside leg top seam
23cm
Template A
inside leg seam
Ankle to crutch measurement
37cm

1 Measure your inside leg from ankle to crutch. Add the measurement to the template above. Copy it on to the paper and cut it out.

2 Make one leg of the chaps at a time. Fold one piece of fabric in half lengthways, right sides together. Pin the template to it. Cut around it.

8cm
37cm
8cm
Template C
11cm
18cm
8cm
33cm
Template D
29cm
13cm
10cm
Template B

1 To make the cowboy hat, copy the templates shown above on to paper, then cut them out.

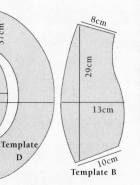

2 Double over the hat felt and pin on the templates, as shown above. Now cut around the templates to make two of each shape.

6 Sew the top of the hat crown on to the sides using large overstitches. This completes the crown of your hat.

7 Take template D and pin it on the stiffening fabric. Cut around it, and then cut out the hole in the centre. This is for the brim.

8 Sandwich the stiffening fabric between the felt brims, and pin. Sew the outside edge of all three pieces together, as shown.

9 Turn the hat crown upside down and pin the crown to it, so the seam ends up inside the hat. Sew them together, as shown.

3 Pin the outside leg top seam. Use running stitch to sew 1.5cm in from the cut edge. Pin and sew the inside leg seam in the same way.

4 Turn the leg the right way out. Following the dotted line on the template, fold over the belt loops. Pin them along the bottom edge, then stitch.

5 Pin and sew the unsewn part of the outside leg seam 10cm in from the cut edge. Make your stitches as neat as possible.

6 Cut fringes into the wide flap down the outside leg, being careful not to cut into the seam. Repeat stages 1 to 6 to make the second leg.

3 The two pieces of felt from template B form the sides of the hat crown. Pin them so that they overlap one another slightly.

4 Sew the two pieces of felt together using running stitch. Pin the remaining free ends together and sew them in the same way.

5 Use one oval from template C. Pin it inside the sides of the hat crown with the side seams at the ends of the oval and the seam outside the hat.

10 Now double the pieces of wool, knot them at the top and tape them to a work surface. Then plait the wool together.

11 Finish the plait by tying a knot at the end. Then wrap the hatband around the base of the crown and knot it.

To look like a real cowboy, wear jeans and boots, as well as a denim shirt, a waistcoat and a bandana. To put on your chaps, pull each leg carefully up over your jeans. Then get someone to help you thread a thick leather belt through the loops, front and back. Don't forget your hat!

Prairie Wagon

The wagons that were used by the settlers travelling to the West were given the nickname of prairie schooners. This was because, when seen from a distance, the white canvas covers of the wagons looked like the sails of schooners (small sailing ships of the time), travelling across the prairie – the wide open grasslands. The wagons were built in Conestoga, a town in the eastern state of Pennsylvania. They could carry weights of up to six tons. The base of the wagons curved up at the back and front to stop the loads slipping out when the wagons were tilted on a steep slope.

In the spring, each wagon train formed into a company of up to 100 wagons. The travellers elected leaders, employed scouts, bought supplies and waited for the good weather that usually came in early May. Then they set off on their difficult journey.

Each day began at about 4 a.m. After preparations were made, the wagon train set off by about 7 a.m. and travelled until 4 or 5 p.m. when it was time to look for a good place to stop for the night.

▲ ROLLING ALONG

Travelling on a wagon was very uncomfortable. There were no roads and the wagon wheels had no rubber tyres, so every bump and hollow in the ground made the wagon jerk and roll. It was far more comfortable to walk, and most people did. The oxen pulled the wagons at no faster a rate than a person walking. Oxen were much cheaper to feed than horses and also much stronger. Pulling a heavy wagon for 3,000km takes a lot of strength and stamina.

◀ PRECIOUS WATER

Water is heavy to carry, so there was usually only enough on a wagon for drinking, to keep people alive. If a wagon train crossed a river or travelled around a lake, then there was water to wash dirty clothes. The soap was handmade from lye (a liquid mixture of ashes and animal fat). The washed clothes were hung on bushes to dry. Sometimes people just put them back on wet.

▲ RUNNING REPAIRS

Settlers expected damage to wagon wheels on the long journey west. The wooden axles on the wheels could be broken if it rolled suddenly into a deep hole or over a large boulder. Most wagons carried at least one spare wheel and tools for making repairs.

KEY	
1 *canvas cover*	11 *cooking utensils*
2 *grease for wheels*	12 *blocks of soap*
3 *tailgate*	13 *stored food*
4 *iron tires*	14 *farming tools*
5 *wooden wheels*	15 *braking system*
6 *oil lamp*	16 *water canteen*
7 *spinning wheel*	17 *packed china*
8 *family Bible*	18 *shotgun*
9 *axle*	19 *jockey box with tools*
10 *milk churn*	20 *wagon tongue*

▲ NIGHT CAMP

Sometimes it took hours to find a safe place to stop for the night. Once the travellers found a spot with some water and shelter, all the wagons were pulled together in a circle. The circle protected the settlers like a round wall. Everyone took a turn at keeping watch while the others slept.

Cowboy Cookout

People were constantly on the move in the West. Native Americans followed the buffalo herds, settlers travelled in wagon trains, and cowboys drove cattle. They all had to carry their food with them or hunt animals for fresh meat.

Cowboys sometimes had very little to eat. Whatever food they had was carried in their rolling kitchen, the chuck wagon. One cowboy had the special job of cooking for all the others. This project shows you how to make the kind of meal a group of cowboys would have eaten on the trail. Dried beans were easy to carry in the chuck wagon, but they had to be soaked before cooking. Chillies are hot-tasting kinds of pepper, and tortillas are a kind of flat, round Mexican bread.

> **You will need:** frying pan; cooking oil; tablespoon; 2 cloves of garlic, crushed; wooden spoon; large tin of tomatoes; sieve; mild chilli powder; dessertspoon; small tins of three different kinds of beans (e.g. kidney beans, butter beans and pinto beans); stock cube; large mixing bowl; 250g plain white flour; 50g cornmeal; salt; knife; warm water; rolling pin; spatula to turn tortillas.

The chuck wagon was stocked with enough food for a trail drive that might last as long as four months. It also carried the cowboys' bed-rolls. Basic stores on the chuck wagon were bacon, beans, potatoes, lard, salt and sugar. The most important thing was the coffee. Everybody drank lots of it, and so the chuck wagon would be loaded with bags and bags of it.

1 Heat 1 tablespoon of oil in a large frying pan until it is warm. Add the garlic and fry it gently until it is soft and golden brown.

2 Add the tinned tomatoes, along with their juice, to the frying pan. Heat them for a few minutes until they are warm through.

5 Crumble the stock cube into the mixture and stir it in. If the mixture is looking too dry, you can add a little water.

6 Keep the mixture bubbling very gently on a low heat while you make the tortillas. Keep an eye on it to make sure it doesn't boil dry.

11 Dust a rolling pin with flour. Roll out each ball of dough into a flat circle. Each tortilla should be the thickness of paper.

3 Stir 1 teaspoon of mild chilli powder into the mixture. Taste it to see if it is spicy enough. If not, add a little more chilli.

4 Now drain the liquid from the three kinds of tinned beans. Stir them in, and warm the mixture through for a few minutes.

Just as they did everything else, cowboys ate their meals in the open air. Every morning and evening they collected their food from the chuck wagon, then crouched on the ground to eat it off tin plates and drink their coffee out of tin mugs. They did not use china plates and cups as these would have been smashed to pieces as the chuck wagon jolted its way along the trail.

7 Now make the tortillas for the chilli. Put 225g of the flour, the cornmeal and a pinch of salt into the bowl.

8 Pour a little warm water into the bowl and mix everything together. Mix in a little more water bit by bit until you get a dough.

9 Sprinkle some flour over a work surface. Knead the dough for about five minutes, until it is elastic. Add water or flour if it is too dry or wet.

10 Divide the dough into six equal portions. Shape them into balls and coat the outside of each ball lightly with flour.

12 Heat some oil in a large frying pan. Place one tortilla in the pan. When the edges curl slightly, turn it over to cook the other side.

13 When each tortilla is cooked, put it on a plate. Spoon some chilli mixture on top and fold it over. Serve immediately.

Why not invite a few friends round for a cowboy lunch? Serve your tortillas and chilli mixture on tin plates, like the ones cowboys used, and drink your coffee from a tin mug.

Western Weapons

The settlers who travelled into the West faced many dangers, and they often carried guns to protect themselves. Wild animals such as bears and snakes might attack them. Thieves might hold up stagecoaches and rob everyone. There was also the fear of a raid by Native American tribes who were angry because their land was being taken away. The people of the tribes did not have guns before the settlers arrived, but they soon traded for them and learned to use them.

There were two main kinds of gun. Hand-held guns called pistols were easily carried in a belt, but they were accurate only over short distances of 50m or so. Rifles were long-barrelled guns that could shoot farther, to distances of about 900m. They could be carried in a sling, hanging from a horse's saddle.

Guns caused many deaths in the West. Native Americans and the US Army fought and killed each other with guns. Robbers used guns to threaten their victims, and sometimes killed people who resisted. People who quarrelled violently sometimes shot one another rather than lose the argument.

▲ PACK A PISTOL
The pistols used in the West were made of metal with a wooden handle, like this one. They carried six bullets in a rotating (spinning) chamber, which led to them being called sixguns. They were big, clumsy, heavy, and very inaccurate.

◄ REACH FOR A RIFLE
A Springfield rifle could fire accurately as far as 1km and was often used for hunting or gunfights. Some rifles had to be loaded one bullet at a time. Others held clips of up to seven bullets and were called repeaters.

▲ BITE THE DUST, PARTNER
No western film would be complete without a gunfight in which the hero rolls around in the dust being shot at by his enemies. In films, the hero almost always wins. This image is from the film *High Noon*.

▲ LONG ARM OF THE LAW
These lawmen were called Texas Rangers, and with all those pistols and rifles, they look like they mean business. States such as Texas and Arizona employed rangers to protect land and towns from gangs of lawbreakers.

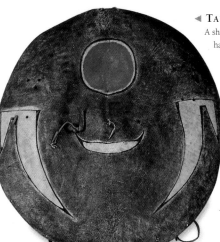

◀ TAKING THE POINT

A shield such as this one would have protected a Native American warrior from the sharp tips of arrowheads or spears. Shields were made from buffalo hide, which was dried, hardened and stretched to make it as tough as possible. Some had soft deerskin covers. Native Americans fought with bows and arrows, spears, tomahawks (war axes) and clubs before they were introduced to guns.

◀ KILLING ME SOFTLY

Among Native American tribes, such as the Sioux, the greatest skill in war did not lie in killing an enemy. Instead, warriors would try to ride close enough to an enemy to touch him with a stick such as the one shown here. It was called a coup stick, and warriors would mark the end of a battle by saying how many enemies they had touched with their coup sticks. This was known as counting coup.

FREEDOM FIGHTER ▶

Geronimo was a famous war leader of the Chiricahua Apaches, who lived in what is now western New Mexico. This photograph was taken in 1887. Ten years earlier, the US government had ordered all Apaches to move to south-east Arizona. Geronimo and half his tribe refused. From their hideout in the mountains of northern Mexico, they fought a war with the US Army, surrendering only after nine years of struggle.

▲ CLOSE SHAVE

Both settlers and Native Americans sometimes cut off an enemy's hair and scalp to prove that they had killed or conquered an enemy. This was known as scalping, and it is shown at the bottom of the picture above. At the top are some ways that scalps were then displayed. Some Native American tribes cut off the whole head of an enemy during war, and kept it as proof of their bravery.

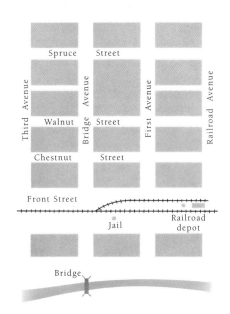

Spruce Street

Third Avenue

Bridge Avenue

Walnut Street

First Avenue

Chestnut Street

Railroad Avenue

Front Street

Jail

Railroad depot

Bridge

Overnight Towns

Although some Native Americans lived in small villages, the land was nearly empty of buildings and towns when settlers first began to move westward. A wagon train on the Oregon Trail, for example, would call at only a few forts on its long journey. Three events were important in bringing towns to the great spaces of the West – the gold rushes, the coming of the railroad, and the great cattle drives.

The first gold rush of 1849 dramatically increased the population of San Francisco. After gold and silver were found in Colorado, Nevada and Arizona, whole towns sprang up overnight as thousands of people rushed to the mines.

When the railways pushed westward, towns such as Denver in Colorado and Dallas in Texas grew in importance because they were near or at the end of the new railroad lines. Then cattle towns sprang up in the areas where the cattle trails ended, near the train stations. Places such as Abilene and Kansas City became busy towns, where cattle were bought and sold, and cowboys spent their pay.

▲ **STRAIGHT AND NARROW**
The streets in many US cities and towns follow a geometric pattern known as a grid, like the one shown here. This is a map of part of Dodge City, a town in the State of Kansas which grew up out of nothing after the Atchison, Topeka and Santa Fe Railroad reached the area in 1872. For the next 20 years it was a major cattle centre. In 1884, almost 8 million cattle passed through it. It also had a reputation for lawlessness, and was known as the Wickedest Little City in the West.

HAUNTED HOMES ▶
Some towns that sprang up suddenly in the West thrived for only a short period of time. At its peak in 1879, the Californian town of Bodie had a population of 10,000 and was a centre of violence and lawlessness. Like many of its kind, it was later abandoned and became a ghost town, with empty buildings and no one living there. Some ghost towns, including Bodie, were restored and are now tourist attractions.

▲ CHEAP THRILLS

Deadwood, in southern Dakota, grew into a town very quickly after gold was discovered in the Black Hills of Dakota in 1876. Almost 25,000 miners poured into the area and Deadwood was where they went to sell their gold and to relax after months of back-breaking work. The town quickly acquired a reputation for violence. It was here that the gunfighter and lawman, Wild Bill Hickok, was shot and killed while playing poker in 1876. He was buried in the same nearby cemetery as another famous figure of the West, Calamity Jane.

▲ FUR FORT

Fort Folle Avoine in Wisconsin was built as a trading post in the wild mountain regions where fur trappers hunted and lived. Before towns grew up in the West, forts were built as places of safety where trappers and settlers could bring goods for sale and buy supplies of food and equipment. The larger forts also had mail offices.

▼ CITY OF DEATH

Some towns were the sites of famous battles, such as the Battle of the Alamo remembered in this painting. The Alamo took place in 1836 in the town of San Antonio, Texas, when a group of almost 200 Texans fought seven thousand Mexican soldiers. Texas was part of Mexico at the time, but many Americans had settled there and wanted their independence.

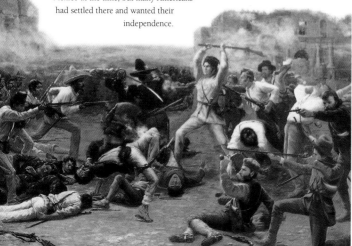

▲ THE ALAMO TODAY

Although some of the settlements that sprang up in the West died out in later years, many grew into successful settlements that are still thriving today. San Antonio is now a modern Texan town, but part of its famous history can still be seen. The old ruined chapel, part of the Alamo fort where the Battle of the Alamo took place, is now a museum and tourist attraction. It commemorates the Texan struggle for independence and the battle which killed 1,500 Mexican soldiers, along with the Texan rebels.

Safe and Sound

Before towns grew up in the West, forts were built as safe places where people could gather together and defend one another. Often the forts were groups of wooden buildings surrounded by a high, wooden outer fence. There was a main gate which could be closed at night or in times of danger. Soldiers, who lived in the forts with their families, defended the settlers against attacks from Native Americans.

Forts were convenient places for wagon trains to buy supplies and equipment on their way westward. Some also had mail offices, where people could receive letters from home and send news to those they had left behind in the East. Often, the only doctor available to settlers was the military doctor in the fort. This project shows you how to make your own model fort, complete with lookout towers and the US flag.

You will need: ruler; pencil; scissors; 2 x A2 sheets of stiff cardboard (for baseboard and walls); household (PVA) glue; 300 wooden lollipop sticks; 2 shades of brown poster paint; paintbrush; A2 sheet of corrugated card (for roofs); 3 x 5cm piece of white cotton (for flag); felt-tip pens; kebab stick; handful of fine gravel; blob of sticky modelling clay.

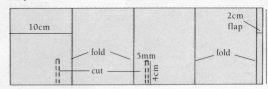

Template A

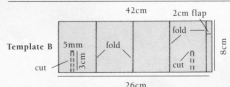

Template B

1 Copy template A once and template B twice on to cardboard, and cut them out. Copy the solid fold lines and the dotted cut lines where marked.

6 Once the lollipop sticks have dried, you can paint them. Dilute some brown poster paint in water to make a thin washy solution.

7 Cut out a 10 x 30cm piece of cardboard. Fold a 2cm flap along the bottom, then glue the flap on to the base, 10cm in from one wall.

11 Cut two 8 x 8cm squares and one 12 x 12cm square from corrugated card, to make roofs. Fold them in half, then paint them brown.

12 The cubes are lookout towers. Glue lollipop sticks to the walls and paint them as before. When the paint is dry, glue on the roofs.

13 Cut a strip of card, 26 x 3cm, and two strips 20 x 3cm. Fold a 1cm flap and glue inside, 3cm from the top. Slot the towers on and paint the fort.

14 Cut a hole for the gateway, 6 x 5cm. Spread the floor with glue and sprinkle fine gravel over the floor.

2 Use a ruler and pencil to measure a large, 30 x 30cm square of cardboard. Cut it out. This will form the baseboard of your fort.

3 Cut out two, 14 x 30cm strips of cardboard. Fold each one in half. Open out and fold a 2cm flap on one side and along the bottom of each strip.

4 Spread glue along the outside of the bottom flaps and press them on to the baseboard. Glue the flaps to fix the sides together.

5 Glue the wooden lollipop sticks to the outside of the fort. Leave a space 5cm wide in the middle of one wall for the gateway.

8 Cut out a 10 x 30cm piece of corrugated card. Glue it to the walls at one end to form a roof. Paint the roof and the inside of the walls.

9 Take the cardboard strips that you cut out from the templates. Fold them along the solid lines. Form each one into a cube by glueing the flaps.

10 Following the dotted lines shown on the templates, cut notches into each cube. The notches will slot onto the walls of the fort.

The finishing touch for your fort is the US flag. Fix your flag in the centre of the fort's courtyard with a blob of sticky modelling clay. The stars on the US flag stand for the number of States. Today there are 50, but in the 1860s there were only 37. The 13 stripes on the flag represent the original 13 States that existed when the USA was founded in 1776.

15 Draw the US flag of the 1860s on the 3 x 5cm piece of cloth – there were 37 stars and 13 stripes! Glue it on the kebab stick.

The Wild Bunch

▲ HIGHWAY ROBBERY
The bandit threatens from behind his bandana. The passengers sit terrified in the stagecoach, staring into the barrel of his gun. Most outlaws used sawn-off shotguns, rifles or carbines (light rifles). The most popular rifle was the Winchester Model 1873, which could fire 15 shots from one magazine.

A lthough few settlers were gun-slinging bank robbers, and most would have never dreamed of robbing a bank, the West did not gain its reputation for wildness for nothing. Some towns and regions were known for violence and lawlessness. Gold- and silver-mining towns such as Tombstone and Deadwood attracted people looking for money to steal, for example. Robbers or murderers running from the law in the East were attracted to the South-west, where its many rocky canyons provided good hiding places, where lawmen found it difficult to follow them. Books and films have since made the names of outlaws such as Butch Cassidy, Billy the Kid and Jesse James, and lawmen such as Wyatt Earp, famous throughout the world.

The West also produced many ruthless people who used force to grab land and power. Some of the rich owners of big cattle ranches, for instance, paid gangs of armed men to drive away small farmers so they could take their land for themselves.

▼ TOMBSTONE TRIGGER
Wyatt Earp is best known for his role in the gunfight at the OK Corral. He was born in 1848 and was a marshal in Dodge City, Kansas, before he moved to Tombstone, Arizona, in 1879, as its deputy marshal. Later in his life he was a saloonkeeper and a prospector. He died in 1929.

► BILLY THE KID
Henry McCarty was born in New York City in 1859 and moved to the West with his mother. His first murder victim was a blacksmith who told him he looked like a girl. McCarty had to run from the law, so he changed his name to William H. Bonney, nicknamed Billy the Kid. He became a cattle thief and a killer – he shot dead at least five men – and died when he was 21 years old, killed by a man who had once been his friend.

THE GOOD OLD DAYS ▶

This is the kind of wild behaviour for which the West became notorious. Four cowboys are so keen to enter a saloon that they cannot wait to get off their horses, but simply ride straight through the doorway! It is unlikely that this picture was based on fact. From the 1880s, when the West became less wild, artists made paintings of scenes like this to satisfy city people who liked to dream about the West, but who had never been there.

▲ TIRELESS TRACKERS

In 1850 Allan Pinkerton founded the Pinkerton National Detective Agency. It used the image of a wide-open eye and the slogan "We Never Sleep" to boast that it never relaxed in its pursuit of lawbreakers. The agency became famous for tracking down criminals and it also uncovered a plot to murder President Lincoln.

STRING 'EM UP ▶

Two swinging corpses show that the locals have taken the law into their own hands. People who do this are known as vigilantes. In parts of the West where there were no regular law officers, groups of vigilantes sometimes hunted down people believed to be guilty of crimes and then killed them, usually by hanging. There was no judge or jury. The victims of this particular incident were 'Cattle Kate' Watson and James Averill, hanged in Wyoming in 1889.

◀ BUTCH AND THE KID

The outlaw Robert Leroy Parker, better known as Butch Cassidy, sits on the far right of the group in this photograph. On the far left is Butch's best buddy, Harry Longbaugh – the Sundance Kid. This was one mean group of men, known as the Wild Bunch. They made a career out of robbing trains, before lawmen chased them so hard that they fled to South America. Butch and the Kid later died there.

Keep 'Em Posted

When outlaws were on the run, posters were printed to warn people to watch out for them. They were called wanted posters because the outlaws were wanted by the law. To encourage people to turn an outlaw in, there was usually a reward. This was a sum of money which you would get if you caught a wanted man or woman. This project shows you how to make your own wanted poster, with a picture and a reward.

In the West, lawmen were known as sheriffs or marshals, and they wore a metal star to show their job was to keep law and order. They came from many different backgrounds. Wyatt Earp worked as a buffalo hunter before becoming a well-known lawman. Tom Bear River Smith spent time in prison before he was made sheriff of Abilene, Texas.

You will need: piece of white paper; pencil; ruler; scissors; tea bag; thick paintbrush; instant coffee granules; photograph of a friend (or cut from a magazine); use of a photocopier; felt-tip pens; household (PVA) glue; tracing paper; very soft pencil (6B).

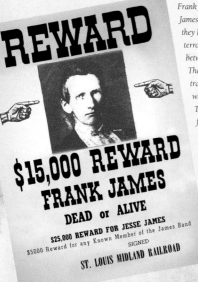

Frank James was Jesse James' brother. Together they blazed a trail of terror through Missouri between 1866 and 1882. They robbed banks and trains, killing anyone who was in the way. The brothers had fought for the South in the Civil War. When the war ended, they would not accept that the South had lost. They saw the banks and trains they robbed as symbols of the North that they hated.

1 Use a ruler and pencil to measure a 25 x 50cm rectangle for your poster on the piece of white paper. Then cut it out.

2 Fold the paper in half lengthways, then in half again. Fold it once more, widthways. Open the paper out again.

3 Carefully tear little strips from around the edges of the paper. This will help to make the poster look old and tattered.

4 Put the tea bag in cold water and swish it about until the water is dark brown. Paint the tea water thinly over the paper.

8 Glue the photo near the bottom of the poster and use the felt-tip pens to draw a border around it. This is the face of the "wanted" person!

9 Photocopy the Wild West characters opposite in sizes suitable for your poster. Decide what to say, then trace the letters you need.

WILD WEST CHARACTERS

A B C D E F G H I
J K L M N O P Q R
S T U V W X Y Z ! ,
0 1 2 3 4 5 6 7 8 9 $

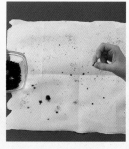

5 Sprinkle the coffee granules over the paper while it is still wet. The paper looks really old now. Leave it to dry.

6 Take a photo of a friend, or cut out a photo from a magazine. Make a photocopy, around 10 x 10cm, and paint it with the cold tea.

7 With the felt-tip pens, draw a border, 2cm in from the edge of the poster. Decorate the corners if you wish.

Make up a nickname for your outlaw. If you want, you can say on the poster the crime he or she is suspected of – cattle rustling, bank robbery, or gunfighting!

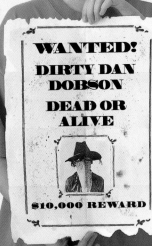

10 Scribble really hard with the soft pencil on more tracing paper. Place the paper over the poster, pencil marks facing down.

11 Lay your tracing of the letters on the scribble tracing. Draw over each one to transfer it to the poster, making your words.

Horsing Around

In the 1800s, horses were an important means of transport all over the world. In the American West, they were very valuable to Native Americans and settlers alike. People could travel long distances quickly on their own horse, or they could use two or more horses to pull wagons, stagecoaches or farm machinery.

There were no horses in the Americas until the early 1500s. The Spanish conquistadors (conquerors) brought the first ones with them in 1519, when they invaded the Aztec lands in what is today Mexico. These Spanish horses probably became the ancestors of American wild horses. Native Americans began to tame and ride wild horses in about 1600 and, by the 1800s, the tribes of the Great Plains were very skilled riders. The people of the Nez Percé tribe bred horses with spotted coats, which are known today as Appaloosas.

▲ PICTURES FOR THE TRIBE
Horses became important to Native Americans both for transport and for trade. They often included pictures of them when they decorated items made for personal use, such as this fringed bag.

◄ BOOTS AND SADDLES
A troop of US Cavalry (mounted soldiers) is crossing a river, every man riding his own horse. Without having mounted Army troops, it would have been impossible for the US government to keep law and order on the Plains. Most Native Americans travelled on horseback and the troops could not have pursued or fought them if they hadn't been on horseback too. In a battle, the soldiers often had a better chance of winning than the Native Americans. This is because they were usually better organized and fought more effectively. Fighting on horseback had been done for centuries in Europe and the cavalry officers were trained to take their enemies by surprise.

WATCH ME ►
Native American tribes of the Plains were famous for their great skills in horse riding. They rode bareback (without saddles), which is a very difficult way to ride, especially if your horse is cantering or galloping. Here four warriors are competing with one another to show who is the most daring rider. Two are riding holding on to their horses' back and stomach with only their legs. This is dangerous to do. If you slip, you fall off and can be hit by your horse's hooves. Skilled warriors could gallop their horses like this and pick something up off the ground without slowing down.

CUTTING OUT ▶

A cowboy on a modern ranch ropes a calf. Sometimes, to rope one of the cattle, a cowboy had to cut it out, or separate it, from the herd. He had to be a skilled horseman to do this. The animal had to be nudged out of the herd and then chased until the cowboy could lasso it with a rope. When the animal came out of the herd, it would run and dodge from side to side, trying to escape the cowboy and return to the herd. Only an excellent rider could swerve his horse to follow the animal and then catch it. Throwing the lasso accurately while riding at speed was also a precise skill that the cowboy had to learn.

◀ RIDE 'EM, COWBOY

A cowboy is riding what was known as a bucking bronco. This was a wild horse that bucked and kicked when someone tried to ride on its back. To tame a wild horse, a cowboy first had to ride it for short periods at a time and hang on while it tried to throw him off. Over time the horse grew used to having a person on its back and would then become a useful horse that would carry a rider all day long. Many of the horses used by both cowboys and Native Americans were born wild. They were descendants of the horses originally brought to America by the Spanish.

BEASTS OF BURDEN ▶

Large, strong horses were a great help to the settlers who carved out farms on the Great Plains. The horses had to be able to pull the special ploughs needed to cut through the thick prairie grass of the region. They also needed to be strong enough to pull the new farming machinery, such as threshers and binders, that farmers began to use towards the end of the 1800s. This horse is working on a modern farm in Colorado.

The Good Earth

When settlers first reached the Great Plains, they thought it would be almost impossible to farm the land. They saw wide sweeps of grassland with very few trees and little water. In summer the weather could be very hot, and in the winter it could be intensely cold, with very heavy snow. It was nearly always windy.

There were few trees, so the first settlers built their homes from turf sods. It was difficult to grow crops because no one had ever ploughed the grasslands before. Slowly, people found ways to solve the problems they faced. They sank wells into the ground for water. They built wind-driven pumps to draw water from the wells. They sowed new types of wheat that grew well in the harsh climate. They bought new ploughs which were designed to be sharp and strong enough to cut through the grasslands. Despite these improvements, though, life was so hard that many settlers eventually gave up and abandoned their farms.

▲ A SOD HOUSE

A small girl lives with her family in a sod house. It is made from blocks of earth cut from the ground by the family's own hands. It took 4,000 square metres of turf to build each house. It was warm inside, but dirty and dusty. Maybe one day, the family might be able to afford to build a more permanent home.

◄ WIND POWER

A wind-driven pump draws water from a deep well. Wind-driven pumps were introduced in the West in 1854, but early designs were expensive. A simpler type wind-driven pump, made of steel, was invented in 1883. It was much cheaper, and soon many farmers had one.

▲ THE FIRST CUT

A team of oxen struggles to haul a plough through the thick turf of the grasslands. When farmers began to plough land in the Great Plains, they said the noise of the first ploughing was like a loud, ripping sound. Along with horses, oxen were the most frequently used transport and farming animals in the West.

◀ MOTHER'S LITTLE HELPER

A woman settler pushes a wheelbarrow loaded with buffalo dung. The pieces of dung were called chips and, when dry, they burned well enough to make a good fire. Because there were few trees on the Great Plains, buffalo chips were the main source of fuel for settlers and Native Americans. Collecting them and hauling a heavy load back home was hard work.

▲ RING OF STEEL

This image is from an 1800s advertisement made to persuade farmers to buy barbed wire. It praises the wire as "the strongest, cheapest and most durable of fence materials". Barbed wire was invented in 1874 by Joseph Gliddon, and soon it was being used everywhere in the West. It allowed farmers to close off their land to stop their cattle and other animals from straying.

▲ STEAM POWER

A threshing machine separates the grain from the stalks of wheat. Steam-powered threshers such as this one began to be used on the Great Plains towards the end of the 1800s. They allowed farmers to thresh grain more quickly and therefore to grow more wheat. The steam engine itself was invented in Europe at the beginning of the 1700s.

◀ RIVER OF GRAIN

Grain harvested from the wheat fields of the Great Plains cascades into a modern-day grain storage tower. Grain from cereal crops, such as wheat, is ground into flour and used for making bread and other kinds of food. Today, the Great Plains are known as the "world's bread basket", because they supply millions of tonnes of grain every year. This fertile region would not exist if it had not been for the hard work of the thousands of settlers who first farmed there.

Patchwork Patterns

To encourage people to become settlers, in 1862 the US government passed the Homestead Act. This promised 65 hectares of land to anyone who paid 10 dollars and lived on the land for five years. Millions of people took advantage of the act and travelled to claim land on the Great Plains, in what are now the States of Kansas and Nebraska.

The settlers had to be very independent. They made most of the things they needed themselves, because they had little money and the nearest shops were usually in towns far away. To keep their families warm, the women made quilts. They used up scraps of old material, sewing differently patterned pieces into a patchwork. The homesteads were often far apart, so women sometimes met up at each other's homes to make patchworks together. These gatherings were called quilting bees and they still take place today. This project shows you how to make a piece of patchwork for a cushion cover.

You will need: stiff card, 15 x 10cm, or plastic patchwork template (from a craft shop); pencil; ruler; scissors; six pieces of patterned cotton fabric in reds, blues and creams, each measuring 15 x 10cm; paper, 30 x 30 cm; felt-tip pen; pins; blue cotton thread; needle; plain blue cushion cover; cushion pad.

0.5cm wide

12cm

6cm

1 Use a pencil and ruler to copy the measurements for the template above on to card. Cut it out.

2 Choose six different patterns of cotton fabric in reds, blues and creams. Make sure the fabrics are the same thickness.

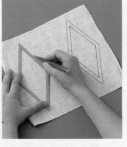

4 On the back of one of the pieces of fabric, use the felt-tip pen to draw around the inner and outer edges of the template.

5 Mark out eight fabric diamonds, then cut around the outside edges. The inner line is the seam edge – do not cut along it!

9 Repeat steps 7 and 8 to pin and sew all the diamonds together along one edge, until the eight pieces form a star shape.

10 Fold the free edges in along the felt-tip lines and pin them. You will be left with a loose corner of fabric at each point of the star.

11 Now use running stitch to sew the pinned edges down. Try to make the edges as flat and neat as you can.

12 Turn the star over and trim off the loose corner of each point. You now have a perfect piece of star-shaped patchwork.

3 Draw around the template eight times to form the design shown above. This is the design for the patchwork.

This woman is sitting beside a collection of patchwork quilts and cushion covers of the kind made in the West. The design on the cushion on the far left is called a nine-patch because it uses nine patches to make the top half and nine to make the bottom half of the central cross shape.

6 Arrange the cotton diamonds on your paper design in the way you want them to appear in the final patchwork.

7 Take two of the cotton diamonds that go next to each other. With the patterned sides facing each other, pin along one edge.

8 Sew the pinned edge using running stitch. Use the inner line that you drew on with the template as a guide for the seam.

13 Pin the star shape carefully in the middle of the plain blue cushion cover. Then sew it on, as shown.

14 The only thing left to do is to put a pad in the cushion cover. Your American settler's patchwork cushion is ready to use.

There are many different kinds of traditional patchwork patterns. You might like to try making a larger piece of patchwork next, or you could design a different shaped template for another patchwork cushion.

On the Warpath

Most Native American tribes tried to find ways to live peacefully with the settlers who came to the West. They made treaties with the US government and agreed to live only in certain areas, leaving the settlers free to farm and ranch on the rest of the land.

In spite of this, there were many difficulties. The thousands of settlers constantly travelling across the land made it hard for the tribes to hunt and live peacefully. Native Americans also had no resistance to diseases such as smallpox which the settlers brought with them, and thousands died. To make matters even worse, the US government did not respect the treaties it had made. It sold the tribal lands to settlers and forced the Native Americans to move to other parts of the West.

After a time, some Native Americans felt that the only way to defend themselves was to fight. Wars between the tribes and the US Army went on for nearly 40 years, as the Sioux, Cheyenne, Arapaho and other tribes attacked settlements, wagon trains and military forts.

▲ SAFE HOUSE
A trader rides in to the safety of the fort. He is relieved to get there after a ride through hostile territory. Even so, the chain of forts built across the West were often attacked by angry Native Americans.

▲ FIGHT FOR LIFE
Native Americans fought with settlers travelling in wagon trains because they wanted to protect their lands. They were afraid that the wagon trains would chase away the buffalo. Sometimes settlers wrongly accused Native Americans of stealing cattle and horses from wagon trains, or killed Native Americans simply because they were afraid of them. Misunderstandings led to pitched battles between the two sides.

◀ MAN OF THE PEOPLE
Chief Red Cloud was one of the greatest warriors and chiefs of the Oglala Lakota, a tribe of the Sioux nation. In the 1860s, Red Cloud forced the US Army to abandon forts on Sioux land. Because of this, he has been called the only Native American ever to win a war.

▲ FIGHT FOR THE FORTS

US troops are attacked by Chief Red Cloud's Oglala Lakota warriors. In the 1860s, the US Army built forts along the Bozeman Trail to protect prospectors heading for the newly discovered gold fields in the State of Montana. Chief Red Cloud fought to keep the newcomers off Sioux land and his warriors attacked the forts. Red Cloud defeated the US Army and signed a treaty at Fort Laramie in 1868. Although Red Cloud succeeded in closing the trail, it was soon replaced by the railroad. Settlers and prospectors continued to pour into Montana.

▲ FETTERMAN DEFEAT

In December 1866 Captain William Fetterman and 80 US soldiers were ambushed by as many as 2,000 Sioux, Cheyenne and Arapaho warriors near Fort Phil Kearny, Nebraska. In the space of about 40 minutes every soldier was killed. It was the greatest military defeat for the US government in the West before the Battle of Little Bighorn in 1876.

TREATY TALKS ▶

Fort Laramie, in what is now the State of Wyoming, was the centre for peace talks between the US government and a number of the Native American tribes who lived in the area. Native American leaders also went to the capital of the USA, Washington DC, and met the US president to try to agree a peace plan.

◀ TRADING PLACES

As well as pushing into the tribes' territory, some white Americans wanted to change the way Native Americans looked and behaved. Many Native American children were taken from their tribes and put into schools, where they were encouraged to forget everything they had ever learned from their own people and trained to be like white Americans. Here, Native American children were photographed before (far left) and after (left) they attended one of these schools. Their dress and whole appearance has changed.

A World of Animals

B efore the settlers came, the Great Plains were full of animals. Beaver, buffalo, deer, rabbits, prairie dogs, raccoons, antelope, bald eagles and armadillos lived there. The Native Americans saw themselves as part of the same world as the animals around them. They took names, such as Sitting Bull, Spotted Tail and Lone Wolf, that described their feelings of kinship with the world of animals.

The tribes of the West valued animals and the things they provided. They made paintings on deerskin, headdresses from eagle feathers, and richly patterned decorations from porcupine quills. The buffalo was the most important animal to the tribes of the Great Plains. They ate its meat, used its hide to make tepees, rugs, shoes and clothes, and carved weapons, tools and jewellery from its horns.

White hunters began killing buffalo in large numbers in the 1870s. They sold the hides to be made into buffalo robes and other leather goods which were shipped to the East for sale. An estimated 30 million buffalo roamed the Plains before the settlers came. By 1900, only 100 survived.

▲ **BUFFALO MEAT**
The hunt is over and the buffalo have been skinned. Now the women hang the meat, cut in strips, over poles in the open air. Once the heat of the sun has dried it, the meat will stay edible for months and can be stored away until it is needed.

◄ **FAMILY DOLL**
Deer and antelope skin was also used to make playthings for children, such as this deerskin doll. The doll was designed to look like a Native American man or woman, so children could play with it and pretend that it was their mother or father.

PLAIN SLAUGHTER ▶
White hunters attack a buffalo. There were a lot of white hunters because of the great demand for buffalo hides, and with rifles it was possible to kill hundreds of animals every day. Back in the time when only Native Americans hunted the Great Plains, they killed relatively few buffalo to meet their needs. The herds of millions of buffalo were in no danger of extinction (dying out). Native Americans knew how destructive the white hunters were being, but no one listened to them. In the end, nearly all the buffalo were slaughtered.

◄ BEST DRESSES

Dresses of the kind these two Native American girls are wearing were made from the skins of animals such as deer and buffalo, which were hunted on the Great Plains. These dresses are very richly decorated and would have been worn only on special occasions such as feasts. Dresses for everyday wear were much simpler in design.

▲ POWER DRESSING

Shirts were often made from deer and buffalo hide and decorated, like this one, with buffalo or sometimes human hair. Designs were painted on to the hide with flat sticks or animal bones dipped in paint made from powdered earth and water. A shirt like this would be a sign that the wearer was an important chief or warrior.

▲ EVERY PICTURE TELLS A STORY

A Native American artist tells a child the story of the tribe's historical events that he has drawn on a deerskin. The skin has been stretched on a wooden frame to make it tight and firm enough to draw on. As well as using animal skin in the same way as paper, for describing and recording events in their lives and history, Native Americans made it into clothes, moccasins (shoes) and tepee covers.

EAGLE WARRIOR ►

Chief Two Moons of the Northern Cheyenne wears a headdress of eagle feathers as a sign of bravery and honour. He led the Cheyenne, who fought alongside Sitting Bull's Sioux warriors at the Battle of Little Bighorn.

Picture Stories

Every year, the Kiowa and the Sioux made pictures to record events that had happened to their people during the year. The pictures were called the winter count, and they were kept by the tribes as important documents. Before the settlers brought paper to the West, the tribes used vegetable dyes to paint the winter counts on deerskin.

In the South-west, Navajo medicine men also made pictures when they wanted to heal someone who was ill. They made the pictures with different coloured, finely-powdered materials, such as sand, pollen or cornmeal. They poured the powder from their hands into intricate designs on the ground. When the healing ceremony was finished, the sand painting was brushed away and destroyed.

This project shows you how to make a sand painting of your own, using coloured cornmeal. It is not easy to pour fine powder through your hands, so it is a good idea to practise before you try to complete your picture. Choose colours that contrast well with one another.

You will need: thick paper, 20 x 30cm; felt-tip pen; 200g cornmeal; four bowls; four colours of powdered paint; four tablespoons; masking tape; fine paintbrush; camera if required.

A modern-day Navajo creates a sand painting. The intricate designs of the sand paintings are decided by the medicine man. He tells his helpers what lines to draw and which colours to use.

1 Draw the design for a simple picture on the paper. You could copy the western landscape shown above if you like.

2 The cornmeal will be the basic material for your sand painting. Divide it up equally among the four bowls.

4 Mix the paint evenly through each bowl of cornmeal. Add more powdered paint if you want to make the colour darker.

5 Tape the edges of your design down on to a clean work surface. You are now ready to begin making the sand painting.

8 Keep going until you have covered one area. You might need more than one handful of paint to complete each part.

9 Wash and dry your hands, then take a handful of different-coloured cornmeal. Again, let it trickle on to the design.

3 Tip two tablespoons of each colour paint into a different bowl of cornmeal. Use a different spoon for each colour.

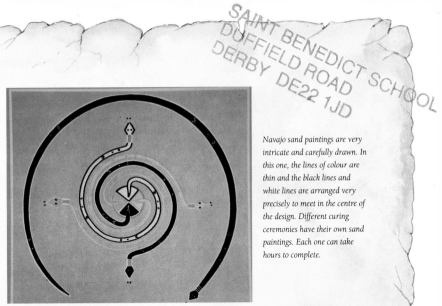

Navajo sand paintings are very intricate and carefully drawn. In this one, the lines of colour are thin and the black lines and white lines are arranged very precisely to meet in the centre of the design. Different curing ceremonies have their own sand paintings. Each one can take hours to complete.

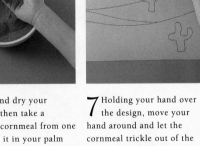

Like North American sand paintings, your picture is not permanent. You could take a photograph if you want to keep a record of it. Alternatively, you could spread glue on the paper before pouring on the sand, to fix the image.

6 Wash and dry your hands, then take a handful of cornmeal from one bowl. Hold it in your palm and make a loose fist.

7 Holding your hand over the design, move your hand around and let the cornmeal trickle out of the bottom of your fist.

10 Use the fine paintbrush to tidy up the edges between each colour. Keep going until you have completed your picture.

Silver Screen Cowboys

Films about the old days of the American West are called westerns, and they have been very popular ever since the film industry began in the early 1900s. This is partly because Hollywood, the film capital of the USA, is in California on the country's west coast. Originally, people chose to make films there because the weather was always sunny and the landscape was so varied.

Back in the early days, before films had sound, Tom Mix was one of the USA's best-known film cowboys. More recently, actors such as John Wayne and Clint Eastwood have also become stars for their roles in westerns.

In westerns made in the past, Native Americans were often portrayed as baddies. However, film-makers have since come to recognize the injustices done to Native Americans in the 1800s. Modern films have begun to show them as strong, independent people who fought for their rights.

◄ SILENT HERO
Tom Mix was one of the first Western stars. From 1910 he made more than 200 cowboy films, at a time when films were made without sound. The words the actors were speaking appeared as written words on the cinema screen. Mix stopped making films after the 1920s, when sound films began to be made.

▼ COWBOY KING
Roy Rogers not only starred in many westerns from the 1930s to the 1950s, he also made records of popular cowboy songs. He was known as the King of the Cowboys, and the parts he played gave rise to an idealized image of the West – one where cowboys were always kind, polite, honest, hard-working and courageous.

◄ SPAGHETTI STAR
Clint Eastwood shot to stardom back in the 1960s for his leading role in a popular series of westerns. The films included *A Fistful of Dollars* and *The Good, the Bad and the Ugly*. In them, Eastwood played a loner who single-mindedly hunted down and killed evil people. Because the films were directed by Sergio Leone, an Italian, they became known as spaghetti westerns. They were made in Italy and Spain.

▲ THE SINGING COWBOY

Gene Autry, shown here with his guitar, began his career as a singer and then became a film actor. He began recording cowboy songs in 1929 and moved to Hollywood to make films five years later. Cowboy songs were so popular that they were combined with films to make musical westerns. These came to be known as horse operas. Because Autry starred in so many musical westerns from the 1930s to the 1950s, he was nicknamed the Singing Cowboy.

▲ HIGH-HO SILVER

The Lone Ranger, shown here with his Native American scout Tonto, was a popular television hero in the late 1950s. The Lone Ranger rode around the West on a pure white horse called Silver, and he was famous for his cry of "High-ho Silver". To hide his identity when chasing robbers and outlaws, he wore a black mask.

▲ REGULAR BAD GUYS

In this still from director Sam Peckinpah's 1969 film, *The Wild Bunch*, the main characters look scruffy and mean. People had become tired of the idealized image of the clean-cut hero, and they wanted more realistic films. *The Wild Bunch* tried to describe what life was really like for the men who had been outlaws when the Old West was less civilized.

THE DUKE ▶

John Wayne was nicknamed the Duke, and he usually acted the role of the strong, silent man who did his duty no matter what difficulties stood in his way. His career in westerns began in 1939 and spanned 40 years and more than 150 films. He was one of the greatest box-office attractions ever in the history of film.

Timeline

The Wild West era started around 1830, when settlers from the eastern USA began to move westwards. Over the next 60 years, nearly three-quarters of a million people joined the flow, forcing the Native Americans out of their homelands. The last battle between the US government and Native Americans took place in 1890.

1600s-1776

1600s-1800 SETTLERS FROM FRANCE make their homes at the mouth of the River Mississippi, in what is now Louisiana. As time passes, these settlers gain control of all of the 4,000km-long river and of the territories on either side of it. France controls almost one-eighth of the territory that is today the USA.

1600s-1830 TREATIES are made with Native Americans, in which settlers promise to respect their land.

1776 THE DECLARATION OF INDEPENDENCE. The US separates from Great Britain. Tension grows between slave-owners and the anti-slavery movement in the US.

1800-1803

1800-1841 THE US GOVERNMENT SURVEYS THE LAND. The new survey encourages more settlers to move west. Some earlier settlers are forced off their land by the newcomers. This results in some politicians demanding that the squatters (people who originally settled on the unclaimed land) should be allowed to stay there.

early US flag

1803 LOUISIANA PURCHASE. President Thomas Jefferson negotiates with the French emperor Napoleon and buys all the Louisiana Territory – 2 million square km. Jefferson has doubled the land area of the young US.

1836

1836 BATTLE OF THE ALAMO on 6 March, in which nearly 200 Texan rebels are defeated by Mexican soldiers in a fierce battle. The Mexican Army had besieged the fort for 13 days before the final onslaught.

1836 MEXICO IS DEFEATED on 21 April by General Sam Houston at San Jacinto. Texas then declares independence.

the Alamo fort in Texas

1840-1841

1840 INDEPENDENCE, MISSOURI becomes the starting point for a trail west, following Lewis and Clark's journey. It leads to the mouth of the Columbia River on the Pacific coast, in Oregon, and becomes known as the Oregon Trail. Although there are other trails west, this is the one used by most settlers.

1841 LAW OF PRE-EMPTION. The US government passes a new law giving people living on a piece of land a first-come, first-served right (right of pre-emption) to buy 65 hectares of land for a small fee. More people move west.

prairie wagon

1843-1844

1843 MARCUS WHITMAN, the evangelist (religious teacher), leads about 1,000 settlers on a wagon train bound for Oregon. This is among the first of the many wagon trains that will follow the Oregon Trail west over the next 50 years. The journey takes between four and six months.

1844 JOSEPH SMITH, MORMON LEADER, IS MURDERED along with his elder brother, as the Mormons are forced out of their home city of Nauvoo in Illinois. They begin to look for a new settlement in the West where they can practise their religion without fear of being attacked.

1854-1859

1854 THE CORPS OF TOPOGRAPHIC ENGINEERS is ordered by the US government to make maps for a transcontinental railroad. Four possible routes are identified.

express train

1859 TELEGRAPH WIRES connect the east coast to the west coast of the USA. At last it is possible to send messages quickly from one side of the country to the other.

1860-1861

1860 B T HENRY designs the first repeating rifle, one that carries five spare bullets and does not have to be reloaded after each shot.

1860 INVENTION OF THE WINCHESTER RIFLE, the most popular gun in the West.

1861 RAILROAD GRANTS are offered to businessmen by the government to persuade them to take part in the building of the railroad. The grant is an offer of land adjoining the route of the track.

1861 CIVIL WAR breaks out between the South (the Confederacy), which wants to keep slavery, and the North (the Union), which wants to abolish slavery.

1862

1862 JOHN BOZEMAN, a gold prospector, finds a direct route east from the gold fields to Fort Laramie. His route becomes known as the Bozeman Trail.

frontier fort

1862 THE HOMESTEAD ACT gives 65 hectares of public land for a small fee to anyone either 21 years of age or head of a family who has lived on and cultivated land in the West for at least five years.

1862 THE PACIFIC RAILROAD ACT is signed by President Lincoln, authorizing the building of a transcontinental railroad.

1867-1868

1867 AT THE TREATY OF MEDICINE LODGE, the southern Arapaho and the Cheyenne are given reservations in Oklahoma. The northern Arapaho are given a reservation in what is now Wyoming.

1868 RED CLOUD signs the second Fort Laramie Treaty, agreeing to settle on a reservation in Nebraska.

1868 GENERAL GEORGE CUSTER leading the US 7th Cavalry attacks a Cheyenne and Arapaho camp in the Washita Valley in the Indian Territory. Over 100 Cheyenne and Arapaho are killed.

1869

1869 THE TRANSCONTINENTAL RAILROAD IS COMPLETED. A golden spike is driven into the track at Promontory, Utah, on 10 May, to mark the joining of the Central Pacific and Union Pacific railroads. The East and West coasts are now joined. A big celebration takes place, with champagne and press photographers. After the celebration the golden spike is removed.

Red Cloud

1871-1875

1871 OVER HALF A MILLION CATTLE are moving up the Chisholm Trail to Abilene.

1874 BARBED WIRE IS INVENTED by Joseph Gliddon. This wire makes it easier for ranchers to fence off their land. Ownership of cattle and land becomes easier to enforce and it is no longer possible to herd huge numbers of cattle across the Plains.

1875 DODGE CITY becomes the main centre for selling cattle in Kansas. It is a major railroad town and a rough place to live and work.

Western town

1804-1806

1804 CAPTAIN MERIWETHER LEWIS and Lieutenant William Clark lead an expedition, ordered by President Jefferson, to explore the country west of the Mississippi. With 40 companions, Lewis and Clark leave from St Louis, Missouri, on 14 May to find a way to the Pacific Ocean.

1805 SACAJAWEA, the famous Native American woman guide, helps Lewis and Clark reach the Pacific Ocean in November.

1806 LEWIS AND CLARK return to St Louis, arriving there in September.

Sacajawea

1820-1830

1820 US MINE-OWNER MOSES AUSTIN is given permission by Mexico to create a colony of 300 English-speaking settlers in the territory that is now the State of Texas.

1830 INDIAN REMOVAL ACT. Many more settlers have arrived in the US and want to own the land that belongs to Native Americans. The US government passes a law taking away the tribes' right to live where they want.

1830 RELIGIOUS LEADER JOSEPH SMITH publishes his *Book of Mormon* in the East of the USA. This leads to the founding of the religion now known as Mormonism.

1834-1835

1834 INDIAN TERRITORY ACT. Many Native American tribes, such as the Choctaw and Cherokee, are forced by the US government to give up lands in the East and go to live in a reserved area known as Indian Territory.

1835 TEXAN WAR OF INDEPENDENCE begins. It is caused by the increase in numbers of English-speaking settlers in the area, who want to be able to make their own decisions without being ruled by Mexico.

Native American war bonnet

1845-1846

1845 TEXAS becomes a US state.

1846 THE MEXICAN WAR breaks out between Mexico and the USA over a border dispute.

1846 ANDREW JOHNSON, future President of the USA in 1865, leads the movement for settlers to be allowed ownership of public land in the West. Other politicians oppose this, believing that land should only be sold, not given as a right.

1846-1862 HOMESTEAD MOVEMENT. People in the East are encouraged by the government to travel west to claim new land.

1847-1848

1847 MORMONS TRAVEL WEST, led by Brigham Young. They colonize the desert wilderness and found what is now known as Salt Lake City, in modern Utah.

1848 JAMES MARSHALL picks up pieces of gold from the bed of the American River in California, starting the California Gold Rush.

1848 END OF THE MEXICAN WAR. The Mexican Army is defeated and, in the Treaty of Guadaloupe Hidalgo in February, Mexico cedes (hands over) 1.3 million square km to the USA.

1849-1850

1849 CALIFORNIAN GOLD RUSH, in which 80,000 people travel to California to find gold, travelling from all parts of the USA and from countries all over the world.

pan used for gold prospecting

1850 TELEGRAPH COMPANIES in the USA number more than 50. The growth of the railroad network makes it necessary to use the electric telegraph to let railroad stations know when a train is due.

1864

1864-68 CHEYENNE AND ARAPAHO WARS. At Sand Creek in Colorado, between 150-500 members of the Cheyenne tribe are massacred by Colonel John Chivington commanding about 1,500 US troops. This leads to all-out war between the Cheyenne, their allies the Arapaho, and the US government.

Sand Creek Massacre

1865

1865 THE NORTH WINS THE CIVIL WAR and slavery is abolished throughout the USA.

1865 FARMERS RETURN TO TEXAS after the Civil War to find that massive herds of cattle are roaming free. Reconstruction of the destroyed towns in the East is creating a huge demand for beef.

1865 ALONG THE BOZEMAN TRAIL, the US government begins to build a road and forts. Many more miners are now using this trail to reach Montana. The Oglala Sioux, led by Chief Red Cloud, attack construction crews and the soldiers sent to protect them.

longhorn cattle

1865-1866

1866 ON THE SEDALIA TRAIL about 250,000 cattle are driven north from Texas to the town of Sedalia, Missouri. Problems with weather, landscape and Native Americans demanding payment mean that only just over 10 per cent of the cattle reach Sedalia.

1866 THE FETTERMAN DEFEAT. A troop of US soldiers defending Fort Phil Kearny, led by Captain William Fetterman, are massacred by the Sioux.

1866 THE US GOVERNMENT NEGOTIATES with the tribes in the Indian Territory and takes away half the land area on which the tribes had been living.

1876-1881

1876 BATTLE OF LITTLE BIGHORN in Montana. US troops move in to force 7,000 Sioux and Cheyenne to return to the Black Hills. General George Custer is killed along with 260 soldiers by a force of 2,500 Sioux and Cheyenne.

1877 CHIEF SITTING BULL, who defeated Custer, flees to Canada to escape government troops.

1881 BILLY THE KID is killed by Pat Garrett at Fort Sumner, New Mexico.

sheriff's star

1885-1889

1885 BUFFALO BILL'S WILD WEST SHOW tours the USA. The show features Chief Sitting Bull, who has been back in the USA since 1881. In 1887, Buffalo Bill takes the show to Europe.

1889 THE INDIAN TERRITORY is swamped by an estimated 100,000 settlers who pour into areas that have been opened up by the US government.

1889 THE GHOST DANCE religion begins among the Sioux. The Sioux believe that this will bring back to life all their people killed in wars with the US government and also the buffalo that have been slaughtered by white buffalo hunters. The US government sees it as a dangerous development.

1890-1900

1890 SITTING BULL IS murdered by government agents. US troops ride into the Native American reservations to stop the Ghost Dance religion. Over 300 Lakota Sioux are massacred at Wounded Knee in South Dakota after they have surrendered to government troops.

Colt .45 pistol

1890 THE TERRITORY OF OKLAHOMA, formerly the western half of the Indian Territory, is officially recognized as a State by the US government.

1900 THE HOMESTEAD ACT has brought more than 600,000 farmers to the Wild West since it was passed in 1862.

GLOSSARY

axle
The pin in the middle of a wheel that allows it to turn.

bald eagle
A large, white-headed member of the eagle family that lives in North America. It is used as a symbol of the United States of America.

bedroll
The blankets and ground coverings that a cowboy slept on. He rolled them up in the morning to carry on his horse's back until he needed them again at night.

bronco
A horse that grew up in the herds of wild horses that lived in the West, which were later captured and half-tamed by cowboys.

buffalo
Large animals, also known as bison, of the same family as the ox. They lived in huge numbers on the Great Plains.

canyon
A steep-sided, narrow rocky valley of the kind found in New Mexico. Canyon was originally a Spanish word.

chaps
The heavy leather trousers that cowboys wear on top of their ordinary trousers to protect their legs from thorns, cattle horns and ropes.

chuck wagon
The covered wagon that cowboys on the trail brought with them to carry the food, or chuck, they needed while they were far away from towns.

corral
A large space enclosed by fencing in which cattle are kept together for short periods of time, often before being sold.

dude ranch
A Western ranch, where people can go for holidays, during which they can live as cowboys of the old West.

fort
A large space, including a collection of buildings, enclosed by strong walls, used to keep people and supplies safe in areas where they are likely to be attacked.

Forty-niner
The name taken by all those people who travelled to California in order to take part in the great gold rush of 1849.

fur trapper
A hunter who travels to wild places to trap animals and skin them for their fur, which he then sells.

gold rush
The sudden movement to a particular region after gold has been found there, by thousands of people who hope to find gold there for themselves.

Great Plains
A vast grassland region stretching east-to-west from the Mississippi River to the Rocky Mountains, and north-to-south from Alberta and Saskatchewan in Canada to Texas.

immigrant
A person who comes to a country to make a new life after deciding not to live any longer in the country from which he or she comes.

kachina
The name given by the Pueblo tribes of the South-west region to the spirits that they believe protect them.

lasso
A long rope that is loosely knotted at one end to make a loop that can be thrown over an object and then tightened to hold it tightly.

lodge
The name given by many Native American tribes to their homes, whether they were homes that they carried with them as they travelled, such as tepees, or permanent homes.

maize
A type of corn that grows naturally in North America and that was farmed by Native American tribes.

marshal
A law officer, whose duties were similar to the sheriff's. He was also a court official.

missionary
A person who travels to a new country to tell the people there about religious ideas in the hope that the people there will make those beliefs their own.

mountain man
A man who, in the early 1800s, lived in the unexplored parts of the West, hunting animals for fur and living and trading with Native Americans.

outlaw
A criminal who hides from the forces of law and order to avoid punishment.

oxen
Large, strong animals belonging to the same family as cattle.

pioneer
A person who sets out to do something no one else has attempted, whether exploring a new country or a new area of human knowledge.

pistol
A single-barrelled, short-range hand gun with a grip, and chamber that holds bullets.

pommel
The raised part at the front of a horse-riding saddle.

prairie dog
A small, burrowing, furry animal, belonging to the same family as rats and mice. They lived on the Great Plains.

prospector
Someone who mines for gold or other valuable materials in the earth, in the hope of making a find and earning money from it.

quill
A long, tough, hollow stalk that grows in large numbers on a porcupine's back. Quills are flexible and can be woven into complex shapes.

raccoon
A small, furry mammal with a distinctive ringed tail and black facial markings, found throughout North America.

rifle
A long-barrelled gun with a shoulder rest designed to shoot over distances of a kilometre and greater.

roughneck
The name given to many of the men throughout the West who worked at whatever kinds of jobs came to hand, such as cattle-driving or building the railroads.

scalp
The skin covering the top of a person's head and the hair growing out of it, cut off by Native Americans and white Americans in war as a sign of having killed an enemy.

scout
A person who acted as a guide and tracker, going ahead of a party of travellers to find out difficulties and bringing back information.

settler
Anyone who went out to the West, found a plot of land, built a house on it and made a permanent way of life there.

sheriff
The name most frequently given to law officers in the West. Sheriffs could be appointed by the citizens of a town or by the county.

smallpox
A deadly, highly infectious disease that caused fever, pustules on the skin and often death.

sod
A large, dug-out piece of earth including the grass growing out of it.

spirit
A non-physical being that people believe belongs to the supernatural world.

squash
A fruit of several different kinds of plant, similar to the marrow family, that Native Americans grew for food. It can be stored for eating for many months after being harvested.

stagecoach
A four-wheeled carriage designed to be driven over long distances pulled by a team of four to six horses. It became the most frequent means of transport in the West before the coming of the railroad.

steamboat
A wide, flat-bottomed boat with a large paddlewheel powered by a steam engine. It was an important means of transport on the large rivers of the West before the 1880s.

steer
Young male cattle, generally aged between two and four years old, bred for the purpose of being slaughtered for their meat.

tattoo
A design, usually permanent, drawn on human skin with needles and coloured ink.

tepee
A tent home of long poles, joined at the top, around which was wrapped a large covering made from buffalo skins. Tepees were the traditional homes of the tribes of the Great Plains, who travelled from place to place, such as the Sioux and Cheyenne.

trail drive
The journey from the regions of Texas, where large herds of cattle were gathered, to the towns further north, such as Abilene and Dodge City, where the railroads from the East began.

trance
A state in which a person does not seem to be aware of the world around him or her but seems completely taken over by a non-physical force.

treaty
Any agreement between two parties in which differences between them are settled on particular conditions.

tribe
A group of families or communities who share a common history, way of life and common ancestors. Native American tribes include the Apache and the Sioux.

vigilante
Any individual who decides to punish someone who they think is a criminal without waiting for a properly agreed court of law to judge whether the suspected criminal is guilty or not.

wagon train
A group of wagons driven by people all going to the same place who have decided to travel together for protection.

INDEX